NORDIC
LIFESTYLE

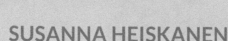

NORDIC LIFESTYLE

Embrace slow living, cultivate happiness and know when to take off your shoes

SUSANNA HEISKANEN

FOUNDER OF THE NORDIC MUM

N❄M

Contents

 # Introduction

When people ask me where I'm from, I always say I'm from Finland, even though I live in Australia. I moved to the UK when I was 23 and then to Australia for work when I was 32. I have maintained my passport, citizenship and connections to Finland ever since I first left for London in 1999. Later, when my kids came, I embraced my identity as a Nordic mum, because I wanted my kids to know the Finnish part of their heritage.

In 2018, I started my website and podcast The Nordic Mum as I wanted to understand what we could do to embrace the Nordic lifestyle more. I used the podcasts to learn more about Nordicness and share it with the people around me. Then when I started researching this book, I looked at my own life and how I still draw from my youth in Finland.

As I explored my heritage by talking about Nordic lifestyle and the people I interviewed on my podcast and writing about it on my blog, I noticed that the content included themes such as sustainability, *hygge*, nature, minimalism and more. I was curious to hear how those people I interviewed saw their culture if they were no longer living in their home country and how they were able to maintain their connection with their Nordic roots. I thought about what I could learn from it. I also talked to expatriates living in the Nordic countries and asked how they found life there.

I wanted to understand the benefits of nature in helping us disconnect and how to live a more minimal Nordic life. How do people in the Nordics manage to spend so much time in pure clean unspoiled nature? Why is nature so important to the Nordic lifestyle? How could I integrate that into my own life?

LEFT: *Finsko, Lapland*

The slow life that the Nordics still enjoy has not been spoiled as the world has become busier and this was something I wanted to explore and make available to all Nordic lifestyle lovers. I admire how Nordic people have been able to sustain the important things in life.

Sustainability is an important cornerstone concept for a good Nordic lifestyle. Many innovations — particularly around sustainability — come from the Nordic countries. Showing how we can make a difference with our behaviour and actions as well as being eco-friendly is expected from everybody in Nordic society.

Since going deeper into these concepts on the podcast, I wanted to ensure that this book would help you honour and embrace Nordic life wherever you are. My aim with *Nordic Lifestyle: Embrace Slow Living, Cultivate Happiness and Know When to Take Off Your Shoes* is to share the life of my upbringing with people who want to connect with Nordic culture and heritage, as well as those who are curious about the differences between Nordic countries.

In this book, I will talk more about the lifestyle and what it means to come from the Nordics and how you can find Nordicness where ever you are. If you want to learn more about Nordic lifestyle, heritage and culture, then this book is for you.

Nordic Lifestyle: Embrace Slow Living, Cultivate Happiness and Know When to Take Off Your Shoes is not about Nordic design, or interior styling the Nordic way. There are other books that you can read on those subjects. It's not a country guide either though I have insights on all Nordic countries. It's also not a cookbook, although I have included some recipes that we use in my house on a regular basis to keep us connected to our Finnish roots. This book is more of glimpse into the life of everyday Nordic people to show you what you can learn from them and what you could implement in your own life.

I hope *Nordic Lifestyle* makes you want to learn more about the Nordic countries. If you do, I have included some resources in the back of this book that will help you to find your inner Nordic.

I would like to thank the amazing people I have had the good fortune of interviewing on my podcast The Nordic Mum. Their insights into their cultures and countries have helped me keep this book factual and understand other parts of the Nordics better.

If you want to learn more about my own Nordic lifestyle, you can join my email list and get to know me better at **www.thenordicmum.com**. I promise not to spam you, but instead keep you company like a good friend. You can also find and follow me on Instagram, Twitter or Facebook for some more Nordic lifestyle inspiration.

Without further delay, let's take off our shoes and enter into this cosy Nordic cabin where a hot drink and a good book are waiting for us by the fire.

Let's learn how the Nordics live and why Nordicness could be the next best thing for you...

PART ONE

DEFINING 'NORDIC'

What does Nordic actually mean?

Imagine you are from the northern part of Europe. No matter which country you think about when I say northern Europe, you no doubt realise that Nordic people have had to put up with a lot to get to where they are today.

Each of the Nordic countries have areas where they excel and things they export overseas. For example, sustainability, FridaysForFuture and the Climate Strike have become synonymous with Greta Thunberg. When you think of the best education in the world, you think about Finland, right? ABBA or IKEA bring to mind Sweden. For many, *hygge* equals Denmark. When asked to imagine Norway, you may think of snow-covered fjords and Iceland recalls those Nordic-style jumpers from a Nordic crime drama.

However cute these images of the Nordics may be, isn't there more to this part of the world than the jumpers? The innovation that comes from Nordics is mind-boggling. Many great inventors and sophisticated processes were originally from the Nordics. Many environmental innovations are from the Nordics too, like green energy from waves, sustainable and eco-friendly fabrics made of seaweed and the use of fish skin in the clothing industry.

People from the Nordics, I think, also feel a companionship with one another. Whenever I have been travelling and come across people from the Nordic countries, I have felt a little pang of belonging. Like the woman I had dinner with at a random restaurant in Ho Chi Minh City in Vietnam many years ago. We had never met before, but we were both dining alone and just started talking. She was from Sweden, backpacking through the area. She had just come across from Cambodia and was on her way to Thailand. We spent the evening talking about

OPENING SPREAD: *Espoo, Finland*
RIGHT: *Steinsdalsfossen, Norheimsund, Norway*

life, travel and missing home. I never saw her again, nor kept in contact, since this was before we had social media. Just talking with her, I remembered home and knew she was feeling the same homesickness as I was, missing the same things, like the snow and the cold climate during the December holiday season.

This meeting was not the only time I've felt this. Another time I saw a man wearing a SISU t-shirt at the Opera Bar in Sydney. I could tell he was not a Finn from the golden tan and sun-kissed hair. After talking with him, I discovered that his mother was a Swedish-Finn married to an Australian and he just happened to get the SISU t-shirt as a present and thought it was a cool word to know.

These meetings with random people have always reminded me of how far we Nordics have travelled and explored the world. However, being Nordic means more than just having a connection with these five North European countries. The countries are tied together with economic, political and cultural ideas too. When Sweden or Finland elects a new prime minister, their first phone calls or foreign trips are to the neighbouring Nordic countries. Our historical ties are strong. The leaders in each country respect and follow similar ideology. Relying on each other's help in times of need is important to Nordic countries, which is strengthened by belonging to The Nordic Council.

Nordic Council being the formal inter-parliamentary Nordic

cooperation among the Nordic countries since 1952 which all Nordic countries and the autonomous areas have representatives.

The people and cultures of the Nordic countries have similar outlooks on life as well. The stillness of society. The no-hurry factor in life. I would argue that slow living is part of us as Nordic people. Perhaps it was created and named in Italy in the 1980s but we Nordics embody this simple way of life by taking it easy and cherishing the important moments.

Since I moved outside Sydney to the south coast of New South Wales in Australia, I have really embraced slow living, becoming more centred in myself, taking those slow walks to taste the air, enjoying the simple things. It has taken me a while to relearn this Nordic way of life after all the bad habits, busyness and looking for the next best thing. My slow life is a work in progress, but I feel more connected to who I am now than when I first arrived in Australia many years ago.

So, how do we define Nordicness? Nordic means many things to many people. For me, it means home. That distant country that I still call home even after all this time abroad. All these peculiarities within my character can be traced to those early years of my life growing up and living in Finland. The outspoken nature, the honesty, the trustworthiness. All that is who and what I am. Nordicness cannot be removed from you.

Here's how you can add some Nordicness to *your* life.

What countries make up the Nordics?

We Finns prefer to talk of Nordic countries, whereas our neighbours like to speak about Scandinavia. So, which countries make up the Nordics? And who belongs to the area known as Scandinavia? Is there a difference? And how are the people different between Iceland, Denmark, Norway, Sweden and Finland? What about the language? There's a lot of confusion around all this, so let's simplify.

The Countries

The difference is that the Scandinavian countries include all except Finland. So that is Denmark, Sweden, Norway and Iceland. Nordic countries are all the countries just mentioned plus Finland.

Finland is not part of Scandinavia, even though people talk about Scandinavia as if Finland were included in that group. Strictly speaking, the Finnish language sets us apart and we are not Scandinavian, but Nordic. To confuse you more term Fennoscandia is used at times when talked about Sweden, Norway, Denmark and Finland.

The basic line is that we all love our neighbours. Unless you mention ice hockey to Sweden and Finland. Or Eurovision to any of the other Nordic countries. There is a friendly competition there. I am sure you get the picture...the neighbour that you love to hate and hate to love, all with good humour, of course.

The Language

Scandinavian countries have the North Germanic (North Scandinavian) language group in common. Finnish, on the other

RIGHT: *Moomin Mug*

hand, is part of the Finno-Ugric language group, which also includes Hungarian, Estonian and the languages used by tribes in some northern parts of Siberia. This separates Finns from our Scandinavian friends, because our language is different.

Most Swedish people understand Norwegian and Danish language. We Finns learn and speak Swedish at school, as it is our official second language. Finns often understand some Estonian and many Estonians can understand and speak Finnish.

Icelandic is different again, as the base of this language is Faroese and western Norwegian dialects.

This may sound complicated, but the truth is that many of the Nordic countries can understand and relate to each other due the similarities in linguistics.

The Islands

Within the Nordic countries, there are islands that do not get mentioned very often. The Faroe Islands, Greenland, Svalbard, Gotland, Lofoten and Åland Islands are part of the Nordics. They might be geographically small (except Greenland), but they have a special place in Nordic hearts for many of us.

The Faroe Islands and Greenland are part of Denmark. However, they are a self-governing archipelago. Greenland is also an autonomous territory of Denmark. Svalbard is a Norwegian archipelago between the mainland and the North Pole. Åland Island is an autonomous island belonging to Finland though physically closer to Sweden. Gotland being largest island on the Baltic Sea belonging to Sweden.

The People

What is the difference between the characteristics of the Nordic people then? I will use some well-known stereotypes here – which might be stretching it! In general, the Finns are a quiet sort and Swedes are considered the talkative ones. Norwegians are commonly considered observant and Danes are said to get

LEFT: *Faroe Islands*

along with everybody. Icelanders are proud and strong-willed.

In this book, I answer how Nordic people are the happiest in the world and dive into how the Nordics live. Given that the darkest period of the year can be pretty miserable, you might wonder how the happiest people can come from the Nordics. And what about summer when the sun does not go down at all and it stays bright all through the night?

As well as discussing the people of the Nordics, I will touch on many aspects of all these countries. Even though I am from Finland and have a Finnish viewpoint, I will be taking you on a journey of discovery what it means to come from the Nordics more widely and exploring how to connect more to this Nordic region. You can have a piece of the Nordic lifestyle for yourself.

To do that, let's first take a look in more detail at some of the more isolated geographic locations.

NEXT SPREAD: *Aleksanterinkatu, Helsinki, Finland*

The Islands of the Nordics

FAROE ISLANDS

This 18 volcanic island group lies 320 km north-northwest of Scotland, towards Norway. The islands are beautiful, isolated and a destination for many who are passionate about bird-watching.

These islands, in the north Atlantic Ocean belong to Denmark. However, though the Faroe Islands are an autonomous territory of the Kingdom of Denmark, if you ask the locals, you'll soon find out that they see themselves as independent from Denmark.

The official language is Faroese, while Danish is taught in schools as a second language.

Although the Faroe Island are connected to Denmark, they are very proud of their independent status. A political wrestle has taken place over Faroese currency and voting in recent years. Changes have been made on how the Faroese people govern their land, though it is still done with the help of mainland Denmark.

The Faroe Islands have recently lifted their status as a tourism destination for those looking for a more secluded part of the Nordics to visit. Bird-watching, especially viewing the puffin colony, is one of the most famous things to do along with hiking, kayaking, fishing and just taking in the rugged but beautiful landscape.

Because of the isolated location, the Faroe Islands are one of those destinations for people who truly want to explore off the beaten track. It is top of my destinations to visit one day and I recommend adding it to your list to visit before the crowds arrive!

GREENLAND

This large island is located between the Canadian Arctic Archipelago and the Nordic countries in the north Atlantic Ocean. It is geographically closer to North America than to the Nordics.

The Inuit people were the first to inhabit Greenland, which nowadays is an autonomous territory of the Kingdom of Denmark.

Inuit people lived in Greenland for centuries before the Vikings arrived. However, the first permanent settlers were the Vikings in the 10th century. There were two colonies established for walrus ivory hunting, which was an in-demand product in Medieval Europe. Hunting continued until the 15th century when the colonies disappeared due to the Black Death and the market for walrus ivory declining.

Today, Greenland and particularly its capital Nook is a tourist and scientific destination. Greenland has an active US military base: the Thule Air Base. There was controversy about the location of a nuclear-powered base US Camp Century that was built on an ice sheet in the late 1950's. Locals did not want a nuclear-powered base on their territory – and with the melting icecaps, you might agree with their reservations! US Camp Century was later abandoned and the buried nuclear waste has become an environmental concern.

Many scientists visiting Greenland have provided analysis about the changes to the thinning icecaps. Over the years, these changes have made locals wary of what is happening to their traditional whaling and hunting of seals and other sealife as the ice disappears.

Greenland offers tours to educate tourists about icecap changes. You can explore icecaps by diving, flying over, skiing or hiking, but you can expect a more sustainable approach than any of these if you're lucky enough to visit Greenland. I would recommend getting there quick, as climate change and the alteration in how the ice behaves will have a lasting impact on the nature that you can view in this part of the world.

ÅLAND ISLAND

This island is nestled between Sweden and Finland and has an autonomous and demilitarised position. It has its own parliament and representation in the Finnish parliament too. The main language there is Swedish and Åland has a distinctive

NEXT SPREAD: *Lofoten Islands, Svolvær, Norway*

Swedish cultural heritage. Though it belongs to Finland, the people on the island call themselves Ålanders.

The capital Mariehamn is known for its slow lifestyle, wooden houses, handcrafts and cafes where you can explore the local life. There are interesting books written about the island and Finnish author Helena Halme has a whole series about a family living there for those looking for a romantic twist on Nordic life.

GOTLAND

This largest island in the Baltic Sea is nestled close to the southwest coast of the Swedish mainland. Gotland has been inhabited since 7000 BC and there are many burial sites along the island that can be traced back to the pre-Viking era. Many silver and bronze treasures from the Viking era have been uncovered and history places Gotland as a significant commercial trading hub for Vikings.

Today Gotland is fully integrated part of Swedish society and an important tourist destination. It is also strategic for the Swedish defence who have had a presence on the island for hundreds of years. If visiting Gotland, you would be astonished by the number of medieval churches the island has and the Viking era buildings that are UNESCO heritage listed in the town of Visby.

SVALBARD

This island group is found between Norway and the North Pole. The islands are the world's northernmost inhabited area and were first used as a base for whalers who sailed far north in the 17th and 18th centuries. After this period, the islands were abandoned.

Later came coal mining, which had an impact on the islands. Nowadays, tourism is encouraged and is one of the main sources of income. Many visit the island to see the rugged glaciers, polar bears, reindeer and arctic foxes. The Northern Lights are visible many nights during the winter and it is somewhere that you can experience the midnight sun, when the sun does not set in the summer skies and shines through out the night. Today, Svalbard is a free economic and demilitarised zone of Norway.

LOFOTEN ISLANDS

The Lofoten Islands lie on the northern end of Norway's west coast. The islands are connected by bridges to the mainland and are known for their dramatic landscape and nature. They are a hive of activity for fisherman and there is evidence that they were settled before the Viking times. You can island-hop and visit many of the beautiful villages of the Lofoten Islands as well as enjoying a visit to the local Viking museums.

I've introduced you to the place, but the Nordic countries and territories wouldn't be what they are without Nordic people. In Part Two, I will introduce you to some intriguing folks who live or have lived in this part of the world, but before I do, here are a few must-know concepts from the Nordic languages that will help you navigate the rest of this book.

 # Famous Nordic words

FIKA (*fi-ka*)

Usually spent with a friend, fika is an afternoon break for pleasant conversation, a cup of coffee and a bun. Used in Swedish companies as a type of meeting, it is frowned upon to turn down invites for fika in the commercial world in Sweden.

HYGGE (*hoo-ga*)

This is a Danish word meaning cosy, being comfortable and feeling content with your life. Hygge is a state of mind more than anything. Hygge can be anything from having a cosy moment with friends over dinner to having a hyggelig time with your family whilst walking in the woods.

LAGOM (*laa-gum*)

Swedes know how to have enough. That is what lagom means, having just enough, just the right amount. Not too little, not too much. This Swedish concept sums up how the Nordics are happy just as they are.

LYKKE (*loo-kah*)

A Danish word for happiness and joy, lykke describes and explains how the Danes are one of the happiest countries in the world.

SISU (*si-su*)

The Finnish word for grit or inner strength, sisu is a kind of perse-verance, stoic determination or ability to sustain courage when facing odds against you. It is a word that you cannot easily translate into English, but something that every Finn knows. There are songs made about sisu and even a tar candy, type of liquorice called Sisu.

MYSIG (*muu-sik*)

This is the Swedish word for being cosy, comfortable and agreeable. The Swedes also say 'giving someone a mysig smile' instead of hygge when describing a lovely moment.

KOSELIG (*koosh-lee*)

Again, this is about being cosy, though it is rather more about togetherness as a group of friends than spending the cosy time alone. In short, the Norwegian word for hygge.

FRILUFTSLIV (*free-loofts-liv*)

The Norwegian concept for open-air living, friluftsliv is all about having a passion for nature, spending time outdoors and living the outdoorsy lifestyle that Norway and the Nordics are famous for.

UTEPILS (*Ooh-ta-pilz*)

Norwegians have a great word for having a beer outdoors. Ute means outside and pils means pilsner or lager. So, let's have a beer outside.

PANTSDRUNK / KALSARIKÄNNIT (*kalsari-kaen-it*)

Those funny Finns, drinking alcohol at home alone in their underwear. Being pantsdrunk means being a homebody, drinking alone until you pass out on your sofa after a bit too much, and mostly bitching about your manager that you do not really like.

PART TWO

WHO ARE THE NORDICS?

Who are the Nordic People?

The Nordics have been inhabited since 8,000 BC. There are some suggestions that this might have been much earlier, perhaps as early as 50,000 BC. Cave carvings and old tools found in Sweden and Norway suggest that hunter-gatherers lived and thrived there. This was around the time when the Ice Age glacier started to withdraw.

When you think about Nordic people, one of the first types of people you may have in mind are the Vikings. Whether it's the very popular television series *Vikings* or the history and artefacts, Vikings epitomise the Nordics for many.

The image of bloodthirsty Vikings who would kidnap women during their raids and drink their enemies' blood from a helmet that had horns on it...historically, they have definitely left a mark and you cannot read about the history of the Nordics without Vikings being mentioned. However, many of the popular culture idealised details about Vikings have been proved non-factual.

I would argue that much of today's life in the Nordics can be traced back to the Vikings. They have certainly given a flavour to Nordic life; for example, Viking marriage was deemed equal with women having more rights than their sisters in Medieval England. This leads me to assume that the equality Nordic women enjoy today started there with the Vikings when women were treated more fairly.

The Viking era was short-lived and ended in 1000 AC, though the Norsemen continued living on settlements such as Greenland and Iceland. The arrival of Christianity signalled the end of the raids for which the Vikings were famous and feared. I talk more about Vikings in the next chapter.

OPENING SPREAD: *Nyhavn, Copenhagen, Denmark*
RIGHT: *Finnmark, Norway*

Of course, people are not as bloodthirsty today as their predecessors. The people of the Nordics are peace-loving and well-known for pushing for a peaceful resolution whatever the conflict may be. They have learned that diplomacy and negotiation are the answer to many political questions that arise.

Many Nordic politicians have made a career in the world negotiating peace and supporting the United Nations on its quest to help those less fortunate countries. For this, previous Finnish president Martti Ahtisaari was recognised with a Nobel Peace Price in 2008 for his career negotiating peace in many war-torn regions including former Yugoslavia and Namibia.

In this section, I will give you a glimpse of the Nordic people, what makes us quirky and interesting, and why so many things are different about us. Next time you meet a person from the Nordics, you might understand us just a little bit better.

When did they rule?

The Vikings ruled northern Europe (present-day Sweden, Denmark and Norway) from around 800 AC to the 11th century. The Viking age was characterised by large-scale raiding, conquest and trading throughout Europe. There is evidence that Vikings travelled as far as Sofia on the Mediterranean Sea, North Africa, the Middle East, and North America.

Who were they?

The Norsemen (as Vikings liked to call themselves) were farmers and fishermen who were interested in travel and exploring the world. They were expert navigators and were able to cover great distances with the use of longboats. They were feared because they stole and traded on these voyages, raiding England's coastline and taking women and treasure back to their homes. Vikings took both free women and slaves as concubines. Their polygamy is believed to have been due to a shortage of eligible women for the average male, leading to the taking of women during these raids. This is not just a myth, but a known fact.

Viking heritage

There are lots of studies showing that Vikings travelled far and wide. DNA tests have confirmed a large proportion of male heritage in northern England comes from the Vikings.

All Nordic countries were influenced by the Vikings. There is also evidence that the Easter Archipelago in Finland was used as a waterway to the east as far as the Caspian Sea. When I was at school, I recall my history teacher telling us that Finns were not Vikings, but peasants, who farmed and traded with the Vikings. New research has shown that there were Viking settlements on Åland Island, debunking the understanding that Finns did not come from Viking blood. However, the debate goes on, as mainland Finns were known mostly trade and guide the Vikings rather than seen as part of the Vikings.

In my experience, we Finns love to think that there is little bit of Viking in us – and not just from being Viking slaves, as many history books have described the relationship between the ancient Finns and Vikings.

Viking myths

Here are some beliefs that popular fiction has strengthened; I was surprised to find that some of these common thoughts about Vikings are not true and find others that were.

Vikings had hats with horns - FALSE

This belief has been disputed and debunked, but popular culture loves to show Vikings with horns in their helmets. I am sure it makes more eye-catching television viewing, but horns were not part of the Vikings' helmets.

Vikings drank blood from their helmets - FALSE

This was not the practice when they celebrated a win over an opponent in a battle, though it is not known how this crept into fiction.

Vikings had slaves - TRUE

They raided many countries and took people to their homes as slaves. Many of the slaves were women so that the Vikings could have concubines and multiple wives at the same time.

Vikings knew how to write -TRUE

Rune stones were left behind as written proof of the Viking stories. These stones are found in today's Sweden, Denmark and Norway. Rune stones had stories written on them in hieroglyphic form, a Viking language you could call it.

Viking women had some rights - TRUE

Women were allowed to marry and divorce in Viking society. They were allowed to take back their dowry (such as animals, parcels of land, linen and wool and even jewellery) in case of a divorce and inherit when their husband died. Women were respected as medicine women and as shieldmaidens fighting alongside with men.

Vikings made jewellery - TRUE

Precious metals were used to decorate weapons as well jewellery. Today's Nordic jewellery design and craftsmanship can be traced back in history to the Vikings.

Vikings travelled the seas in longboats - TRUE

There are lots of examples in today's Nordic countries of how ship-making and boat-carving was inherited from the Vikings. Many of today's boat designs have Viking influence.

What happened to the Vikings?

A question I have often wondered about is what happened to the Vikings. When I was researching this book, I was surprised to learn that the answer is not that the Vikings got the plague and died. The Norsemen continued to live in Nordic countries in areas where they settled.

It was the introduction of Christianity that forced Vikings to stop their raids. Many churches along the northern coast of England were relocated inland making the raids impractical, because they required travel by land rather than boat.

At the same time, areas that had been raided in the past became better equipped to defend themselves from the Vikings. The raids were not as financially successful as they had been and were abandoned in 1066 AC, when the Norwegian King Harald was defeated and killed in battle attempting to claim part of England. This is described as the end of the Viking era.

Although the Viking age came to an end, the Royal Houses of Norway, Sweden and Denmark can be traced back in history to the Vikings.

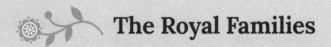

The Royal Families

There are three Royal Houses in the Nordics. All the Royal Houses are related or connected to our ancestors. In fact, the Danish Royal House is one of the oldest monarchies in the world.

The Royal House of Norway belongs to the House of Glücksburg. The members of the Norwegian Royal House are Their Majesties King Harald and Queen Sonja and Their Royal Highnesses Crown Prince Håkon, Crown Princess Mette-Marit and Princess Ingrid Alexandra.

The Swedish Royal House is the Royal House of Bernadotte. The Swedish Royal House includes King Carl XVI Gustaf, Queen Silvia, Crown Princess Victoria Duchess of Västergötland and Princess Estelle Duchess of Östergötland. The Swedish Royal House also includes Princess Victoria's other children and the sister and brother of Princess Victoria, Princess Madeleine and Prince Carl Philip and their children.

The Royal Danish House Schleswig-Holstein-Sonderburg-Glücksburg is related to the Norwegian Royal House. The royal family consists of Queen Margrethe, Frederik Crown Prince of Denmark, Mary Crown Princess of Denmark and Prince Christian of Denmark. The other children of Mary and Frederik, and Frederik's brother Prince Joachim and his children are also part of the Danish Royal Family.

Making the Royal Houses accessible

The people love and respect the royals. They are seen more as modern royals who work and make good rather than just cut ribbons. All the royal families, more so the Swedish Royal

LEFT: *Rosenborg slot, Øster Voldgade, Copenhagen, Denmark*

House, have become increasingly relatable to average people and have worked to find common ground.

I still recall a childhood story told by one of my uncles, who met the King of Sweden in the street in Stockholm. He was just a child at the time, but he did not believe that it was the King of Sweden when he introduced himself! Kings did not just walk around in the streets! This just shows that the Royal Houses and their members tend to be more accessible to the public than perhaps their relatives in England.

Although all Royal Houses still have the status symbol, they remain strongly supported by the people. Of course, there are calls for modernisation on the part of the public, cutting costs and removing some of the less important aspects of the job as well as some of the less public members of the Royal Houses.

Current situation

The drive to modernise has resulted in a drop in popularity for the King of Sweden in recent years. There are calls for him to step back and give way to Crown Princess Victoria. Calls for a change of head of the Royal House has been strong in Denmark and Norway too.

The royals work with diplomats, supporting foreign trade and making their country better known in other parts of the world. Their travel promotes opportunities and is an asset to the country.

Although calls to reduce the number of royals have been supported by tax-payers, I believe there is a place to make them more useful for the country.

The Royal Family that did not happen

So, what about Finland then? During Finnish independence in 1917, there was support for Finland to become a monarchy. Finland looked to Prince Frederick of Hesse from Germany to take the crown and offered him the Kingdom of Finland.

RIGHT: *Kungliga slottet, Stockholm, Sweden*

ABOVE: *Örebro Slottet, Örebro, Sweden*

He was elected on 9 October 1918 and, as the King of Finland, he was given the slightly more Finnish name of Fredrik Kaarle. His full title was Charles I, King of Finland and Karelia, Duke of Åland, Grand Duke of Lapland, Lord of Kaleva and the North.

Prince Frederick was seen, in the eyes of the monarchist government, as an ideal candidate for Finnish king. He came from the House of Hesse dynasty, which had existed since 1264. He was the brother-in-law of Kaiser Wilhelm (monarch of the powerful German Empire) and his wife, Princess Margaret of Prussia, was a granddaughter of Queen Victoria.

Finns believed that the German Empire would defend Finland against possible attacks from Russia, hence the monarchists favouring a monarch with German ties. However, German ruler Kaiser Wilhelm abdicated his throne on 9 November 1918, two days before Armistice Day, and Frederick abdicated his own crown as King of Finland one month later on 14 December, by which time he had never set foot on Finnish soil.

Abdication was likely due to political pressure and a change of heart on the Finnish side. It would not have been favourable for a German prince to rule in Finland as Germany lost the First World War. Sketches made for the crown to fit the King were never finished and a Finnish monarchy was short-lived though still remembered in the history books.

Did you hear about a Kingdom of Iceland?

I was fascinated to read about the story of Iceland signing the 1 December 1918 Act of Union, an agreement with Denmark that recognised Iceland as a fully sovereign state, an independent country from Denmark though sharing a monarch. Hence a Kingdom of Iceland.

The monarchists went ahead and the Kingdom of Iceland established its own flag and coat of arms. It asked that Denmark represented its foreign affairs and defence interests on its behalf. The Act would be not be reviewed until the 1940s, finishing in 1947.

King Christian of Denmark was ruler from 1912 to 1947, and the only King of Iceland. In 1944, while Denmark was still under German occupation, Icelanders voted to sever all ties with the Kingdom of Denmark and to found a Republic of Iceland. Thus, Christian's title as King of Iceland became void.

History tells us that King Christian did not much like the outcome of the vote. However, at the urging of his relative, the King of Sweden, King Christian begrudgingly accepted it. He sent a message of congratulations to Iceland during the celebration of the founding of the Republic on 17 June 1944.

Despite his acceptance of Iceland's independence, Christian never stopped using the title King of Iceland and continued including it in his regal name until his death in 1947.

So, all five countries of the Nordics have had Royal Houses at one point in time, albeit sometimes for very short periods!

Famous people from the Nordics

Nordic people have achieved many incredible feats and there are so many I could have included here. However, I wanted to cover some of those that I feel have given something to the world. You might have heard of them; some might be completely unknown to you.

ALFRED NOBEL (SWE)

Alfred Nobel invented dynamite in 1864, but he is remembered for the Nobel Peace Prize established in his name and in accordance with his wishes upon his death in 1888. A lesser known fact is that he holds 355 patents to his name. The Norwegian Nobel Committee gives out the Nobel Peace Prize and subsequent awards every year. The awards ceremony is held in Oslo, Norway even though Alfred Nobel was Swedish by birth. Why, you might ask? Alfred Nobel wished for the Peace Prize to be administered in Norway, which was ruled by Sweden at the time of his death.

GRETA GARBO (SWE)

Greta Garbo is a Swedish actress who is remembered for such melancholic and tragic performances in the Golden Era of Hollywood as Anna Karenina and Mata Hari. She later lived a reclusive life in New York after turning her back on Hollywood and the public eye. Many stories are told about Greta Garbo being seen in public parks in New York just minding her own business. She lived in the same flat for the rest of her life after moving to New York and passed away surrounded her servants who she had remembered in her will.

INGRID BERGMAN (SWE)

Another Swede famous for her roles in Casablanca and For Whom the Bell Tolls, which earned her an Oscar, Ingrid Bergman was hailed as one of the most beautiful actresses of her time affording her lots of admirers. The Oscar-winning superstar was ostracised from Hollywood for nearly six years due to her love affair with director Roberto Rossellini while she was still married.

BJÖRK (ISL)

Björk is an Icelandic singer-songwriter, record producer and DJ, whose most notable hits include It's Oh So Quiet and Big Time Sensuality. She is known for her eccentric outfits and her stark ethereal voice but she is also a classically trained pianist whose first album Björk was released 1977 when she was a teen. She is still recording and has a cult following on social media.

VIGDÍS FINNBOGADÓTTIR (ISL)

The first woman in the world to be elected president in a democratic election, Vigdís Finnbogadóttir of Iceland served from 1980 to 1996. She was known for her forward-thinking opinions and action for female rights, as well as being a single mother of a daughter during her presidency. This was unheard of at the time, though far less controversial today.

JEAN SIBELIUS (FIN)

Jean Sibelius was a Finnish composer and notable for his Kalevala symphony and Finlandia hymn, both much-loved and admired. He was one of the few artists in Finland to receive a government grant back in 1898 to remove any money worries so that he could concentrate on his music.

TOVE JANSSON (FIN)

This author, novelist and painter is known for her Moomin characters and animations. Her partner Tuulikki Pietilä produced the animations for her books, which were written on an island off Helsinki where they spent most of their summers together. Tove Jansson and Tuulikki Pietilä lived in flats connected by a rooftop so that they could continue to see each other away from the public eye. Their relationship was a public secret that was not talked or written about in the press.

ALVAR AALTO (FIN)

Alvar Aalto was a 1930s Finnish architect, designer of glassware, furniture and textiles. His most famous piece is the Savoy (Aalto) Vase that can be seen in many Finnish homes today. He was a clever businessman, founding Artek back in the 1930s. Artek specialised in selling furniture, lighting and accessories designed by Finnish and international designers.

HANS CHRISTIAN ANDERSEN (DEN)

This Danish writer of plays, novels and poems is best remembered for his fairy tales that have been translated into over 120 languages. The Little Mermaid, The Ugly Duckling and The Emperor's New Clothes are his notable works. These classic children's stories are still being read today and have been adapted for the small screen as animations.

KAREN BLIXEN (DEN)

Karen Blixen was a Danish author who wrote her books in English and Danish. Her most famous book was Out of Africa that was adapted as an Oscar-winning movie with Robert Redford and Meryl Streep. Out of Africa covers Karen's life and her affair with Denys Finch Hatton, son of a titled English family after her divorce from her husband in the 1920s. This was quite a shock in 1920s society, and she was shunned by many on her return to Denmark to write, when she was ill. She was nominated for the Nobel Prize for Literature several times, though she never won.

ROALD AMUNDSON (NOR)

This Norwegian Antarctic explorer successfully reached the South Pole on 14 December 1911. However, he could not reach the North Pole and had many failed attempts at doing so. He was the first person to sail through the North-West Passage, the first man to reach the South Pole and the first to take a trans-Arctic flight across the North Pole. His story has been translated for movies and television series.

HENRIK IBSEN (NOR)

The Norwegian playwright and theatre director Henrik Ibsen was hailed the founder of modernism in theatre. His notable plays are A Dolls House, The Enemy of the People and Peer Gynt.

JO NESBO (NOR)

Author and former soccer player Jo Nesbo's books have been translated into over 50 languages and sold over 50 million copies. He is best known for his crime novels featuring Inspector Harry Hole. He is seen as part of the Nordic noir literature movement, which I'll cover later in Part Three.

EDWARD MUNCH (NOR)

A Norwegian painter, Munch's best work The Scream is an iconic image of the art world. Well-recognised anywhere you go is the agonising face in the painting, said to symbolise the anxiety of humans in the modern world.

Saami People

Who are the Saami people?

Before the Vikings, the Saami people inhabited the Scandinavian Peninsula. They speak a or Saami, a group of Uralic languages. Today most of the Saami people are bilingual and speak Saami as well as the language of their location (Finnish, Swedish, Norwegian or Russian). For example, ethnic Saami groups like Skolt Saami speak Skolt Saami and live in Sweden, Finland and Russia. It should be noted that there are nine Saami dialects, and some differ from each other so much that people from different dialects do not necessarily understand each other.

Where they live

Saami people are the only indigenous people of the Nordic countries and are not only recognised but protected under the international conventions of indigenous people. The Saami people inhabit northern parts of Norway, Sweden, Finland and the Kola Peninsula in Russia.

Religion

The traditional Saami religion was a type of polytheistic paganism. However, as Saami covers a large area of land, there has been an evolution of variations in beliefs and practices between different tribes. The dominant religions among Saami people are now Lutheranism and Russian and Eastern Orthodox.

Clothing and style

The traditional Saami clothing is called gákti, which according to Polarpedia was made from reindeer leather and sinews in

LEFT: *Jokkmokk kommune, Sweden*
NEXT SPREAD: *Birtavarre, Norway*

past times. Now it is more commonly made from wool, cotton, or silk. Women's gákti typically consists of a dress, a fringed shawl and boots or shoes made from reindeer fur or leather. The boots often have pointed or curled toes.

Traditional gákti are most commonly seen in variations of red, blue, green, white, medium-brown tanned leather or reindeer fur. The colours, patterns and jewellery of the gákti are indicative of where a person is from, whether the person is single or married, and sometimes even a specific family.

Customs

The Saami handicraft, known as duodji, originates from when the Saamis were self-supporting nomads. They held the belief that an object should first and foremost serve a purpose rather than being primarily decorative.

Yoik/joik is a feature of Saami musical tradition. Yoiks are song-chants and are traditionally sung a cappella, usually slowly and deep in the throat.

Reindeer herding is a strong part of the Saami culture and ancestry. Today, this practice is legally protected as an exclusive Saami livelihood in Norway, Sweden and Finland.

Saami today

There is lot that can be said about how Saami people were treated over the years. Truthfully, not very well. However, reconciliation for past wrongs is taking place, including returning artefacts to their rightful home, as well as recognition of the importance of the Saami culture and support for people in maintaining their culture, language and connection to the land.

Many argue that Saami have been instrumental in enriching our culture and that we should be more proactive in supporting and protecting Saami culture and people. Some say that the tourism industry is ripping off Saami heritage by selling cheap replicas of their dresses and performing Arctic-Circle-crossing ceremonies that have no meaning for Saami people.

More needs to be done and it remains to be seen how the governments in each of the Nordic countries tackle the issue of reparations. It is promising to see many vocal Saami people taking up Saami issues in the media and driving change in local government around Saami decision-making powers, especially around how nature and the land on which they live is protected for future generations.

How foreigners experience the Nordics

When I interviewed guests on The Nordic Mum podcast, other people's experience of the Nordics was a recurring theme. I was interested to hear how people experienced my homeland from an outsider perspective. Were we unique, somewhat distant, quirky, weird or just plain bland?

I recall one of the conversations I had with Japanese businessman Daiki Yoshikawa. His view was that Finnish and Japanese people have lots of common. People in both countries love their personal space. Look at the queues at the bus stop, for example, he laughed. People have more than few metres between themselves! He also noted that both cultures have a habit of being very quiet. And he's right. We Finns can be uncertain if we like something or not and don't give away our emotions easily - somewhat similar to Japanese people, apparently.

When I was talking to Paola, an Italian mum of three and author who had lived in Finland for over 20 years, her frustration on getting Finns to open up was palpable. I could relate as I felt the same way when I was back home. In Finland, I find getting your friends and family to warm up enough to talk openly and show emotion takes some time. Like...a few days! It's like the kind of effort we use when heating a smoke sauna...It will be okay in the end, but you have to feed it lots of wood first.

I can only imagine what it is to live in Finland when, let's face it, small talk does not really exist. If you talk too much, you are considered too chatty; if you do not talk enough, you are considered shy or rude. Paola had formed relationships with other expats more than with locals. Again, a common theme with many people that I have spoken to on the podcast.

Swedes are no better at forming attachments and relationships according to author and a Finnish father of one Jesse Karjalainen. He moved back to Sweden after living in Australia and the UK for most of his adult life. He said it was difficult to make friends with Swedes, even though he spoke the language and was able to feel comfortable in his surroundings. As he put it, the Swedes did not let him in.

Let's face it, the pandemic has not helped any of this. Jesse told me the small talk was awesome, but you would never get your foot in the door, be invited to coffee, dinner or anything else, because you were considered a 'foreigner', because of your accent and/or background.

What about living in Iceland? Satu Ramo, author and social media personality, has lived there nearly 20 years, got married and had children. She found Iceland an easy place to live. She said the first time she arrived in Iceland to learn the language she knew she had come to the right place. She was able to tune in to the culture, through her studies, language-learning and hanging out with locals. She is still living local Icelandic life years later.

Helen Russell, an English journalist and author, lives in Denmark and her take was that the outdoorsy lifestyle and rough-and-ready approach was what surprised foreigners most about the Danish. She has been in Denmark with her husband and kids for a few years and her kids now speak Danish. Originally from England, Helen had not lost her identity but embraced the Danish way of life and even wrote a book about it called The Year of Living Danishly. In it, Helen was on a mission to uncover the key to Nordic happiness, which I will also cover in Part Five of this book.

My take on all of this is that the Nordic nations can be closed off. People from outside the Nordics tend to need to work little bit harder to get into any circles than they would in other cultures and countries. Knowing the language and customs can be helpful, though. Many people in the Nordics speak English and are helpful, but for you to get most out of life in the Nordics, you need to embrace Nordicness and learn the local tongue.

Equality

When I moved to London to work there as a nurse in 1999, I felt like a fish out of water. The English were very polite and half of the time they would say 'pardon?' when they did not understand you, which sounded like French to me. I had difficulty understanding them.

When I started going out with my now-husband, I was lost with his North Yorkshire accent. There were so many things I wanted to tell him but I struggled to find the words. From me, he learned only a few words of Finnish at first (and even then mainly swearing), but he did start to recognise some more of the Finnish language over time.

When I spoke in English, he was often confused who I was talking about as I always got 'she' and 'he' mixed up. I still do! As I like to tell people, I cut the balls off men by calling them 'she'! Why do I mix these up so much? Well, in the Finnish language, there is only one word for she/he which is *Hän*. You can have a conversation about someone without knowing if they are male or female. You might even call them 'it'. And that is alright by Finns.

Equality is not just within the language. Through the centuries, women of the Nordics have been seen as equal to men. If you look at Nordic mythology, the national identity of the Nordic countries is a female figure. Going back in history to the Vikings, as I mentioned before, women were allowed to divorce and could get their dowry back. This meant that they were independent and were able to establish themselves and move on with life. In Medieval times elsewhere in the world, this was unheard of. Medieval England, for example, was a very different place where a man 'owned' a woman and what they brought into the marriage. Divorce did not exist there at that time.

Living in the UK gave me some perspective on how good things were back home! Free education, equal treatment, the same rights in the work place, parental leave, etc. The list goes on. I never realised I would not get to enjoy these benefits as I was only going to stay away for a few years for work experience and then move back to Finland. However, here I am living in Australia some 20 years later.

Moving to Australia was another shock... I was expecting the workplace to be similar to the British style with the same values. Many of the social systems were started by the Brits, right? Unfortunately, I was mistaken.

Don't get me wrong, I have happily stayed at home looking after my sons for many years. Yet here in Australia, when I did want to return to work, it was impossible. Childcare is not subsidised by the government like it is in the Nordics. You are expected to arrange this on your own and pay for it as well. There is no support network like we have at home in Finland and women are expected to go back to work full-time from the get-go. Flexibility in the workplace is something Australians could and should aspire to achieve.

I now understand why so many of my mum friends here in Australia decided not to return to work and stayed on long maternity leave that turned into years out of the work force, focusing instead on lovingly looking after their children, husband and homes.

In the **Global Gender Equality report,** the Nordics are frequently in top place led by Iceland. I have taken for granted for so long that women can access health care, politics and work, and have a say that is respected. Since working and living in Australia, I have come to question these basic rights for women. In most of the Nordic countries, usually almost half of the members of parliament are female. This is unprecedented in Australia. Most of the Prime Ministers at the Nordics at the time of writing this (2022) are female.

The way to change this is to vote for more equal treatment at work and in life generally, to make more noise, demand better treatment and jump on the opportunity to do so wherever you are.

The Nordic countries were not the first to give general voting rights to women: New Zealand did this as early as 1893 and countries like Austria and Russia gave women the right to vote in the 1910s. However, Nordic sisters have it good and many countries could still do much better.

My take on equality between the sexes is that it is a basic right. We should all expect the same, no matter where we live. However, the only way we will get there is by voting in people

History of equality in the Nordics

FINLAND
- Finland was the first country in the world to extend the right to vote and stand for elections to all women and men in 1906 one of the most ground breaking reforms at the time.
- Finland was also the first country to elect women to Parliament: 19 were elected to the 200-seat Parliament in 1907.

  Today, there are more female ministers than male ministers in the current government (2022) led by Sanna Marin.

SWEDEN
- Women in Sweden were granted suffrage in local elections in 1718.
- In 1842, girls were allowed to be educated in schools that used to be restricted to males only.
- In 1919, women gained full voting rights.

NORWAY
- In 1911, the first woman held office in the Norwegian parliament.

who are willing to adapt and make changes. Nordics are also one of the most open and progressive countries when it comes to LGBT rights. They have been forefront on removing stigma and prejudice against LGBT people.

Next I'll explore what makes Nordics Nordic, what makes them different to some other countries in the world and what is similar between the Nordic countries.

- Universal women's suffrage was passed in 1913.
- The equal pay principle was agreed in the 1920s.

ICELAND

- In 1917, women were granted the same rights over their children as men.
- In 1920, the age barrier to voting eligibility for women was removed entirely.

  Iceland is top in most of the surveys about gender parity and equal pay.

DENMARK

- Women in Denmark gained the right to vote in 1915.

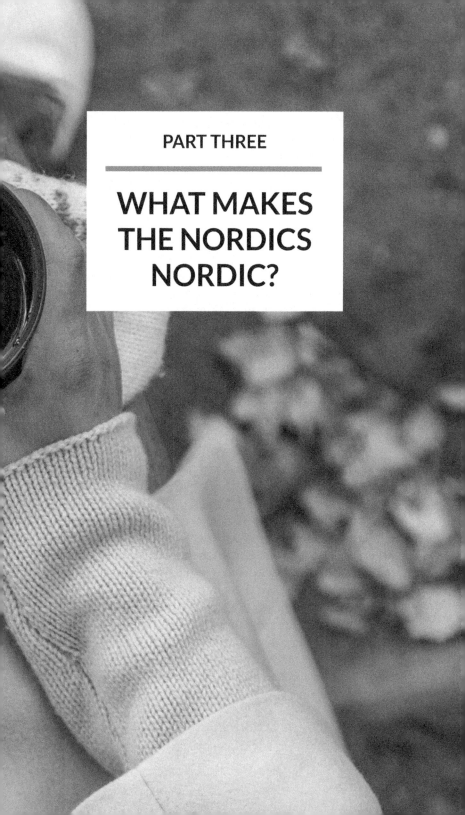

PART THREE

WHAT MAKES THE NORDICS NORDIC?

When I light up a candle at home, take a deep sigh and land myself on the sofa to read a book and listen to my favourite music, I feel contentment. This is hygge. I am back in the Nordics right in that moment.

This feeling reminds me of so many things about home.

My granny always had candles burning on the table. It was like you could not have dinner without a candle. For me, it came to be a mark of cosiness, a homely feeling. You do not need to celebrate anything to light a candle. They just make you happy.

Another reason I love reading so much is the library system. Having a public library system that works means you can do research as a student, borrow books for your own leisure and just enjoy the architectural masterpieces that libraries are in the Nordics. You almost feel like you would want to live among the books. That is how cosy the libraries are!

There is a lot to be said about *hygge,* Nordic noir, ABBA, pole walking and Absolut vodka. These words and concepts are known around the world and are connected with the Nordic countries. But what is it that makes the Nordics so unique and different? Is it the weather? The people? The nature? The outdoorsy lifestyle?

Nature and the cold climate are certainly one aspect that characterises Nordicness. Summer, when the sun does not go down, can be long and hot. Then there is the harsh and even longer winter, when you just want to have a sauna at the end of the day and enjoy a hot drink by the fireplace.

The weather makes the Nordics unique. The cold has not stopped people living and thriving. I always get asked about the weather. What do people do when it is -30°C outside? Like do you still go out? Well, yes we do. We just have layers of clothes on and dress sensibly for the weather. We have different weather gear for each season. Here on the Australian east coast, it does get

as cool as 10°C in winter. While this could be a summer's day in Iceland, I'm still amazed that people go out and about in summer shorts and t-shirts. When they realise it's too cold for that, they often stay inside instead of wearing adequate clothing to go out!

Kids in the Nordics play outside in any weather. They have adjusted to the hard conditions and make the most of the daylight in winter. Come summer, you can hardly get people to stay in. That's when we top up our vitamin D and enjoy the other extremes of weather.

Sports are all year round. Over winter, we go skiing, cross-country or downhill, and enjoy anything to do with snow. When the season changes, we take up walking, hiking, biking, orienteering and other types of sports enthusiastically.

Nature changes with the season and you have different animals to look out for, explore and record. Nature photography is a popular hobby and many people have cameras just in case that moose is crossing the road in front of them at just the right time.

The outdoors – both nature and weather - has really shaped the national identity of Nordic countries. Even our mythological creatures are animals or drawn from the shape of an animal-like creature.

Still, our national identity is more than just an animal or a flower. Nordic people are taught at school about the *meaning* of the emblem and what it has lent to our identity over the years. We love sports and sports stars are well-regarded in society. They are put on pedestal alongside pop, rock and heavy metal stars. Sport brings up rivalry between countries, but it also unifies people across borders.

Next, we'll learn about Nordic celebrations, sports, what makes the Nordics Nordic and how all Nordic countries have a unique national identity as well as what that tells us about them.

Celebrations
at the Nordics

All the Nordic countries have their own quirky celebrations, but many are celebrated across the whole region. Here, I have picked a mix of my favourites as well as those where I still remember to mark the occasion even while living abroad.

Midsummer

This Pagan celebration has strong roots in all the Nordic countries and is characterised by the endless midsummer sun when the sun does not seem to go down at all. Otherwise known as the Summer Solstice, Midsummer was always a celebration of fertility and long-awaited life returning after winter. The celebrations were originally developed for John the Baptist and took place on 24 June. Nowadays the festivities surrounding that date and Midsummer's Eve is celebrated throughout all the Nordic countries.

Some of the Pagan rituals are still observed today and many are believed to have come from the Vikings, who were superstitious and would pray to Viking gods Freyja and Freyr for a better harvest the following year. Pagans would carry out certain rituals during Midsummer. They believed that the presence of evil spirits was strong during the longest day of the year, so they would light huge bonfires to ward off dark forces.

Midsummer celebrations in Sweden and Finland

Midsummer is often celebrated with a bonfire and people drinking and throwing barbeques. Usually, we get together in a summer cottage near the sea or lakes away from the cities.

NEXT SPREAD: *Sognsvann, Oslo, Norway*

In Norway and Denmark, the celebrations are similar with bonfires and picnics by the sea.

In Sweden, celebrations include a Midsummer pole (*midsommar*stång) decorated with flowers and leaves that people dance around and greenery placed around houses for good luck and prosperity. *Midsommar* is an official holiday, taking place every year on the closest Friday to 23 June. Many Swedes flock to the countryside for *Midsommar* where you often find them enjoying a typical Swedish picnic laden with pickled herring and other local specialities.

The Summer Solstice festivities continue all day long with singalongs to the Swedish drinking song *Helan g*år, and shots of vodka or *aquavit*, as is the tradition.

There is a Nordic saying: if a girl picks seven different flowers in the silence of the Midsummer night and puts them underneath her pillow, she will dream of her future husband.

Meanwhile in the rest of the Nordics

In Iceland, *Jonsmessa* you can expect something different to what you might see in Sweden and Finland. Although many spend time with family and friends, you might find them at a Summer Solstice music festival. The celebrations are more superstitious than religious. One such belief is that healing stones will float up in lakes and ponds; rolling around naked in the morning dew is also said to have incredible health benefits.

In neighbouring Norway, celebrations are always on 23 June every year no matter what day of the week. Midummer's Eve is celebrated with good food, music and dancing, and the burning of huge bonfires. Bonfires have survived as a ritual since Viking times, when it was believed that the fire had special cleansing powers, and was also used to drive away evil powers, including witches.

Denmark also enjoys their Summer Solstice festivities on 23 June every year. During their Midsummer (*Sankthansaften*) bonfires, many Danes will toss witch effigies made of twigs and cloth into the fire. Like in Finland and Norway, this is to make sure that evil spirits are kept away.

Easter in the Nordics

Witches with sticks appear on your doorstep demanding candy...you might think it's Halloween, but, no. This is Easter in the Nordics. Particularly in Finland, Easter witches are let loose to gather sweets. If you do not have any to give them, you will be cursed with bad luck. If you do, you get good luck of course.

In Sweden, Easter is slightly different, although the Easter witches are still on the loose here too. The focus is instead on opening up and cleaning out the family summerhouse. At this time, Swedes still feast on sweets and traditional holiday foods — herring, salmon, root vegetables — and may indulge in spiced schnapps around the dinner table.

In Norway, the tradition is more about the Easter egg hunt for kids. Adults will often have Easter breakfast prepared with eggs and pancakes.

In Denmark, friends and family members make paper snowflakes, marked with riddles and signed with dots in lieu of the sender's name. The receiver of the 'teaser note' then has fun trying to guess who sent them the letter. If they guess correctly, they receive a chocolate egg for a job well done. The game dates back to the 1600s and is still going strong each Easter.

In Iceland, Easter means chocolate eggs and more chocolate eggs! There is an Easter egg hunt on Easter Sunday followed by a feast, including lamb and sugar-glazed potatoes.

As you can see, every Nordic country has similarities for Midsummer and Easter celebrations, but what about Christmas?

Christmas

In Nordic countries, Christmas is celebrated in the evening of 24 December, on the eve of Christmas Day. This is when Father Christmas (Joulupukki in Finnish) comes to bring presents, which are laid under the Christmas tree. And you actually get to meet Father Christmas! You also get together for Christmas dinner with family, have a sauna and visit the graveyards of loved ones to leave a candle for those who are no longer with you. Cemeteries look magical around Christmas time with the candlelight against the snow.

Christmas has many names in the Nordic countries: Joulu, Jul, Jol or Yule, which come from the Pagan holiday of Yule. Although it is a Christian tradition celebrated on the 24 December, it is based on the days-long feast that was perhaps the most important celebration of the year, the Winter Solstice. Yule marked a turning point in the calendar, the longest and darkest time of the year before the New Year and the start of a new season when days started getting longer.

Santa Lucia and Advent

All Nordic countries begin Christmas early by celebrating Advent. First Advent is at the end of November and is when we make the Advent wreath of spruce and red berries and light the first Advent candle of four. One candle is lit every Sunday leading up to Christmas.

In Sweden, Denmark, Norway and Finland, 13 December marks the Santa Lucia's Day celebration. There are church services and girls in white dresses with a wreath and four candles. This celebration used to be mostly for Swedish-speaking people in Finland, but is now celebrated all around the country.

The Gnome, Joulutonttu, Nisse or Yule Lads

The gnome has many meanings in Nordic folklore, but there's a specific one at Christmastime...

In Finland, the *joulutonttu* peeps through the windows to see if the kids are naughty or nice and reports back to Father Christmas, who Finns call *joulupukki*.

In Sweden, Norway and Denmark, Nisse the mischievous gnome starts visiting kids 12 days before Christmas, leaving presents for them in their slippers.

Meanwhile, in Iceland, there are 13 mischievous Yule Lads who arrive on the 13 nights leading up to Christmas. They come one by one and leave a potato instead of presents if children have been naughty. Stories of Yule Lads are told to scare kids into behaving nicely in the run-up to Christmas.

The Christmas Goat or Joulupukki

Christmas goats are made from straw as Christmas decorations for the Christmas table. The goat has its origins in the Pagan god Thor and his chariot-pulling goats. The old tradition says that the goat was transformed into a character who punishes people for not cleaning their house ready for Christmas.

Later the Christmas goat transforms into *Joulupukki* aka Father Christmas. This is translated word for word from the Finnish phrase Christmas goat. Father Christmas brings presents to children like elsewhere in the world, but is named Joulupukki for Finns who celebrate Nordic Christmas. *Joulupukki* lives in Korvatunturi, which is in the Finnish Lapland we all know. That is where he takes his sleigh and greets children from all over the world.

The Christmas Sauna or Joulusauna

Joulusauna is taken on the evening of 24 December. You gather together with your family before the dinner to clean yourself. Sauna is also a way of freeing bad spirits. It is thought that the saunatonttu spirit would punish you if you misbehaved. Even today, kids are told to be nice or the saunatonttu would come. So that you keep saunatonttu or saunagnome happy, you offer him some Christmas porridge on a plate that you leave under the seats of the sauna.

Christmas food

Every Nordic country has their own delicious food for this season, but there are similarities among them. Gravadlax (cold smoked salmon) is eaten in all Nordic countries in different forms. There is plenty of meat on the table too. In olden days, the meat would be cured, smoked or dried when served but today the Christmas feast consists of roasted pork in Norway, Denmark, Sweden and Finland, and smoked lamb or grouse with berry sauce in Iceland. There are lots of different kinds of pickled herring eaten at Christmas, along with rye bread, and carrot and swede casserole in Finland.

This feast is bigger than Thanksgiving in the US. The food usually lasts a few days after Christmas when you make soups from the leftovers or freeze whatever you can to eat later.

Other Celebrations

FINNISH INDEPENDENCE DAY

You cannot miss the Finnish Independence Day celebrations on 6 December. The day is celebrated with military honours and a military parade. Again, people take candles to the graveyards to remember their loved ones and the day ends with a three-hour handshaking marathon with the President, which is televised.

BEER DAY IN ICELAND

Is it 1 March? Then it must be Beer Day in Iceland. Every year, Icelandic people mark the end of beer prohibition, which was 74 years long, from 1 January 1915 to 1 March 1989. And yes, you drink beer. Lots of it.

NORWEGIAN NATIONAL DAY (SYTTENDE MAI)

This is observed on 17 May every year and commemorates the constitution of Norway that was signed on that day in 1814 at

LEFT: *Top view of a table full of traditional Swedish Christmas food*

Eidsvoll. This constitution declared Norway an independent kingdom from Sweden.

The day is remembered with children's parades in most of the cities. There are market stalls with hot dogs, ice cream and other food. In addition to flags, people typically wear red, white and blue ribbons. Some wear a traditional outfit called a *bunad*.

The Royal Family makes an appearance on the balcony of the Royal Palace. The day is about gratitude for freedom, equality and brotherhood among Norwegians.

DANISH NATIONAL DAY (GRUNDLOVSDAG)

Celebrated 5 June for the signing of Denmark's first and current constitution, this is not even an official holiday. However, the majority of the workforce in Denmark have a half-day off work and many shops and businesses shut after midday.

There are no street parades or festivities, but often picnics in the park with family and friends eating *pølser* (hotdog) and drinking beer, followed by some group singing or *fællessang*. The same day is also Father's Day in Denmark.

SWEDISH NATIONAL DAY OR FLAG DAY

This commemorative day is celebrated on 6 June as the foundation day of Sweden. The tradition goes back to 1916 and the Stockholm Olympics where Flag Day was created in memory of King Gustav Vasa who become King of Sweden in 1523. Some have argued that the day marks the end of Kalmar Union (the union between Norway and Sweden) hence it is the independence day of Sweden. The day is a public holiday there.

All over the country, there are celebrations with Swedish flags in every nook and cranny. Folk dancing, flag making, historic performances are all part of the day, as is an appearance by the Royal Family, who travel to Skansen an outdoor museum by horse carriage wearing traditional costumes. The King gives a speech and the citizenship ceremony is observed for those chosen for the honour.

Libraries

When I lived in Finland, my solace was always the city library. I loved the smell of books, the thrill of finding something I hadn't read before. We even had a library bus that brought books for people who were not able to get to the city library. You would get in the bus and borrow the books you wanted from there.

The Nordic library system

Libraries have been and continue to be one of the best ways to immerse yourself in the culture of the Nordics. Finland's Library Act made all library services free and open to everyone and sought to promote equal access to civilisation and culture, lifelong learning, and active citizenship and democracy. As a result, the country as a whole has quite the soft spot for libraries and was ranked the most literate nation in the world in 2016. Oodi Helsinki Central Library being an architectural masterpiece where you can borrow not just books but space to work and even 3D printers.

Reading and using library services does not end there. Iceland boasts a high rank in its number of authors and readers. One out of every ten Icelanders has published a book. For a small population of mere 350,000, this is a lot.

Ad ganga med bok I maganum.
Icelandic saying meaning: everyone gives birth to a book.

Sweden is a nation of readers as well. Over 60% of the population uses public library services. In Norway, like in many Nordic countries, the library service includes electric bikes, guitars, hammocks and more. You can also borrow a person. For real! In the Human Project, you can talk to a person and listen to their life story for 30 minutes. Each of these people have a label like 'unemployed', 'bipolar', 'refugee' and so on. The goal is to fight prejudice.

A law passed in 1985 stated that every county must have a library available for its citizens. In Denmark, there are unmanned self-service library services available for the book worms. Some are dementia-friendly environments; some have a no-children policy. As you can imagine, there is a library for every need in the Nordics.

Readers and writers

Nordic people love to read and write books. I am no exception. The start of this book was based on reading lots of books during the pandemic lockdown in Australia. The more I read, the more I was convinced that there was a book in me that needed to get out.

I could not find a book like the one you are holding, covering the Nordic countries and explaining their culture like I have done here. If you are looking to learn more about the Nordics, I have a book list for you at the back of this book with other resources to help.

RIGHT: *Stockholm, Sweden*

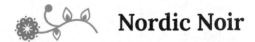

Nordic Noir

Have you seen Wallander? Or The Killing? Or perhaps you have seen Bordertown? Or heard of the Millenium Trilogy, Lisbeth Salander and The Girl with the Dragon Tattoo? These all are Nordic crime series or movies. Some based on books, some not. This style of Nordic crime writing has had a huge following since the 1990s.

Henning Mankell's books on Kurt Wallander are said to have been the start of this genre. This detective series was adapted into film and television and made people want more Nordic crime on television and in books.

What is Nordic noir?

The Nordic noir genre represents a tension between the still and bland society in the Nordic countries and the darker side of crime. It often includes murder and rape, with racism and misogyny as the underlying reasons for the crimes.

Nordic noir is critical of the society in which the series is based. The complex mystery usually involves politics and the main characters are not without flaws. They have their own issues and demons to make the antihero more relatable for the viewer.

How does Nordic noir differ from other crime series?

Critics have said that Scandinavian crime series are more "realistic, simple and precise... and stripped of unnecessary words". The antihero is usually a police detective worn down by their career, who will cast a light on the flaws of society, which are usually the reason for the crime itself. The antihero may use questionable methods to resolve the crime. There are many strong main female lead characters too, like Lisbeth Salander.

How does Nordic crime look visually?

A description of Nordic noir is a slow and melancholic pace with multi-layered storylines. As per Wikipedia, Nordic noir often features a mix of "bleak naturalism and desolate locations, with a focus on the sense of place where bad things can happen."

These were the distinguishing emotions of the series *Bordertown* that were combined with an atmosphere arising from the fear of Russia.

Other examples, Stieg Larsson's Millennium Trilogy deals with misogyny and rape, and Henning Mankell's faceless killers focus on Sweden's failure to integrate its immigrant population. Both adaptations to the big screen and television were hugely popular

especially in the Nordics but abroad as well. The authenticity of these dramas have had audiences hooked on the television series.

These series also borrow something from Scandinavia's political system. The apparent equality, social justice and liberalism of the Nordic model are seen to cover up dark secrets and hidden hatreds. Nordic life is portrayed in Nordic noir as imperfect and more rational and relatable.

Why Nordic noir is loved by audiences

Realism is compelling and forms a basis for the generation of antiheroes, social critique and realism. If you look at Wallander from the 1990s, it describes a social democratic class society and the antihero fighting against it. Lisbeth Salander is a feminist hero fighting class-based chauvinist misogyny. This strong female lead character is captivating to audiences as is her fight for justice.

Finally, Nordic TV crime dramas are so different from action crime dramas that are characterised by car chases and fist fights. You know what you can expect in a crime drama.

I recall reading Stieg Larsson's Millenium Trilogy in 2005 in Swedish as I wanted to experience the book in its original language. I was translating from Swedish to English with an English dictionary while reading. It took me long time to read, but in the end I was glad I did. The Swedish movie version of the books makes more sense to me than the English one!

Dramas like *Wallander* are often slow-paced with not much happening, but are usually well-written and well-acted. In addition, they often have a brooding and atmospheric quality, along with superb cinematography.

If you want to have a visual feast, check out more television and movie recommendations at the back of this book.

 # Sports-Mad Nordics

If you give a Nordic person skis, they will beat you on them! If you give them a stick, they will win at ice hockey! Anywhere in the Nordics where you mention sport, there will be an enthusiastic conversation. Sport keeps people together as much as it divides them though.

Here is what you can expect each nation to be watching... Finland's number one sport is ice hockey together with other winter sports such as cross-country skiing. In the summer, Finns may be found playing *Pes*äpallo.

Ice hockey is also played in Sweden, while in Norway people are more into football, cross-country skiing and ski jumping. The Danes love football and are pretty good at it. Just look at their success in the World and European Cups! Handball is also big in Denmark and Iceland, where it is a popular pastime and a national sport.

PESÄPALLO AKA FINNISH BASEBALL

This Finnish version of North American baseball was invented by Lauri 'Tahko' Pihkala in the 1920s. Many Finnish expat communities have brought it to other parts of the world as well, but in Finland it is considered a national sport.

ICE HOCKEY

Mainly played in Sweden and Finland, both countries have produced many NHL (National Hockey League) players for the North American league. Each country has won the European and World Championship titles several times.

FOOTBALL (SOCCER)

All the Nordics love football and it features heavily as a school sport and hobby. Every Nordic country has been in European Championships except Iceland.

HORSEBACK RIDING

Popular in all the Nordics, particularly in Iceland. There is something wild about galloping on Icelandic horses on the sea shore with the wind blowing through your hair. If you ever get there, you'll want to try it.

WEIRD SPORTS

Want to go off-piste on the sports front? The Nordics have the weirdest sports you'll find... like, the wife-carrying world championships where you tackle an obstacle course with your wife on your back, swamp football literally playing football in a swamp, the sauna world championships (no longer operating), air guitar and mosquito squashing to name a few. Yes, these all are done in Finland.

Since 1901, the Stockholm Ice Yacht Club of Sweden has been fast racing ice yachts across frozen lakes and fjords.

Underwater rugby and also rinkball are popular in the Nordics. Rinkball began in Sweden in the 1950s and is played on the ice hockey rink. Players use an ice hockey stick to hit a bandy ball. Underwater rugby is played in the shallow end of swimming pools. The balls are filled with saltwater to keep them from floating to the surface.

Whatever the sport, Nordics love the competition and being outside no matter what the weather.

HOW TO SPEND TIME OUTSIDE

Skiing is a popular sport in most Nordic countries. There are council-made ski tracks in every little village, around every ice-covered lake and city park. The exception is Denmark, where they do not take to the skis.

RIGHT: *Haifoss Waterfall, Iceland*

Hiking is another popular pastime. Again there are marked treks that you can take everywhere. They are signposted and you can stop and enjoy a moment in nature, make a fire, cook some sausages and have a hot drink before continuing. Many take a trip to Lapland during *ruska* when the leaves start to change. You can best explore Lapland's beautiful colours by hiking.

Nordic pole walking is pretty much walking with ski sticks in your hands but without the skis on your feet. Nordic pole walking took the world by storm a few years ago. Everyone was walking with sticks in cities and in the countryside. Nordic pole walking is seen as great exercise and a good way to keep fit especially for older people as the sticks help support you and you use your arms not just your legs. Snow shoe walking is another sport that has gained popularity in recent years.

My mum sent me ski poles while I was living in London many years ago and my boyfriend refused to walk with me in the local park if I had the poles with me! I quietly put them away, taking them out only when we went for long hikes where there wouldn't be many people around. They are pretty handy for balancing and you do see them being used by hikers.

As Danes do not ski or hike, what do they do to get outside? They **bike**. There are so many great biking tracks around Denmark, and as the country is mostly flat, it makes it even more fun.

Many use a bike as a way to get to and from places, like work, university and school. The cycle lanes are a familiar sight in and around cities in other Nordic countries too. During winter, you need to bike with care, as icy and snowy tracks can be treacherous. But winter is not really an obstacle to do anything, right? I remember biking to university in -30°C, just like most of the other students did.

Thank you for the music

Not everyone in the Nordics is a heavy metal fan. I'll just repeat that again. Not everyone in the Nordics is a heavy metal fan. It might look and feel like it, but no. Heavy metal is a major genre in the charts in Finland, for sure, but if we look at other Nordic countries, we see a different music scene.

Sweden has produced some of the best popular culture bands in last few decades. If you have not heard of ABBA, Roxette, Ace of Base and the Cardigans among others, you must have been living under a rock. A heavy metal rock!

Norway had its heyday with A-ha in the 1980s and today DJ Alan Walker is the best export in the music business from Norway.

Denmark's best-known musician overseas is songwriter and record producer Lars Ulrich. He rose to fame as the drummer and co-founder of American heavy metal band Metallica. You might have also heard of the 1990s Danish pop band Aqua or rock band Gasolin'.

Björk Guðmundsdóttir, known simply as Björk, is an Icelandic singer-songwriter. Her unique voice and distinct songs are well-known and loved. Her heyday was during the 2000s but she is still active and touring.

What about Finland then? Most Finnish music success is from heavy metal bands like HIM, Nightwish, Apocalyptica, Rasmus and Children of Bodom. You also have more recent exports like Saara Aalto and Alma, who are making waves in pop.

EUROVISION

You need to see Eurovision to believe it. How to describe this once-a-year music extravaganza? All Eurovision countries send participants to the host nation to sing and there's a vote on the winner. Counting the votes always takes ages and there are

always controversial performances that receive nil points. Of course, there are also amazing performances and outlandish outfits that leave you wondering...what the heck?

Eurovision has a strong following in the North. Sweden won the very first Eurovision with ABBA singing *Waterloo*, making the band an overnight success all over the world. Since then, all the Nordic countries have won the competition at least once except Iceland.

There is friendly competition between the countries. You follow which neighbour gave you points and which did not. We still love our neighbour even if they gave us nil points.

There are Eurovision parties in people's homes where we eat meatballs and gravy and chips. We cheer for our country and fly our flags. Needless to say, the Nordics enjoy Eurovision banter and the winner is an instant celebrity in their country. (Just don't mention Lordi.)

Okay, I mentioned Lordi, so I will tell you about this Finnish heavy metal band that won in 2006 wearing monster masks. The band brought Lordi mania to Finland. The mask-wearing monsters were the most extreme example of a Nordic Eurovision winner. Most winners have been more traditional pop music performances.

Traditional music of the Nordics

Every country has their own specific instruments that are considered the basis of their folk music. Accordion has been considered a folk instrument in Finland since the 1800s. The accordion was played in cafes, on the streets and at spontaneous gatherings of people. It was considered even too common to be a folk music instrument like kantele, which is the traditional Finnish and Karelian pluck-string instrument.

In Sweden, folk music was accompanied by *nyckelharpa*. This has the look of a violin but keys are attached to tangents to serve as a fret and change the pitch of the string. The nyckelharpa hangs from your neck as you play it in front of you. These are still used today as part of the folk music movement and you can study the nyckelharpa at the Royal College of Music in Stockholm.

The *Hardanger fiddle* is a traditional Norwegian instrument that looks like a violin but is made of lighter thinner wood and has eight to nine strings. The Hardanger fiddle was used on the soundtrack of the Lord of the Rings trilogy movies.

All Nordic countries enjoy varied types of popular music and folk music is seeing a revival with many local bands using traditional instruments or folk-type singing.

Folk music is a vital part of Nordic celebrations like Midsummer and there are festivals dedicated to the craft of folk music in each country. In school, kids are introduced to music with the traditional instruments and you learn to play and sing traditional music which has a strong hold in the Nordic culture.

10 things the Nordics have given the world

You might have heard of some of these institutions or all of them. Suffice to say, without Nordic innovation and creativity, the world may be a very different place. How many of these have you used or owned?

IKEA (SWE)

What can I say except that you would recognise this blue and yellow furniture store anywhere? It has everything you could want or need to decorate your home. It is Nordic design that is also cheap and very practical. Just don't forget to have some meatballs when you are visiting.

I recall my first home together with my husband in London. Everything was from IKEA, as it was what we could afford. In London in the late 2000s, we were still using the white garden chairs that my in-laws bought from Singapore IKEA in the 1980s.

ABBA (SWE)

ABBA transformed popular music when Waterloo won the Eurovision Song Contest in London in 1974. They went on to become one of the most popular bands in the history of pop music. This best-selling Swedish band has sold an estimated 385 million copies worldwide. If you have not heard and danced to Dancing Queen some time in your life, you have not really immersed in the Nordic life!

HEART RATE MONITOR (FIN)

The heart rate monitor was invented in Finland in 1977. The wireless heart rate monitor was originally a training aid for the Finnish National Cross-Country Skiing team in the form of a watch with built-in capability to record the pulse of the person wearing it. We now use smart watches with heart rate monitors in fitness, training and everyday life to monitor and record progress.

LOUDSPEAKER (DEN)

Peter Laurids Jensen, dubbed the Danish Edison, experimented with a recorder and speaker, then in 1915 built the first coil loudspeaker. The Magnavox speaker was first launched in San Francisco. It played Christmas carols in front of 75,000 people.

CHEESE CUTTER (NOR)

Most Nordic countries use the Norwegian cheese cutter (also sold in IKEA) invented by Norwegian furniture maker Thor Bjørklund. He patented the 'Ostehøvel' in 1925 and established a factory in Lillehammer.

The Norwegian cheese cutter is in use in other European countries like Switzerland, the Netherlands and Germany. You might have seen one or you might own one without realising that it is originally from Norway.

XYLITOL (FIN)

Even if you haven't heard of xylitol, there's a good chance you've encountered or consumed it. It is made from birch tree branches found in Finland. Xylitol is an alternative to sugar used to prevent cavities, plaque, pneumonia, osteoporosis, and ear infections in children.

Found in many popular brands of chewing gum, candies and butter substitutes, it is sold mainly in the Nordics, but is finding its way out to the world as an alternative sweetener in foods.

SMS (FIN)

It's hard to imagine a world without texting these days. Mobile phones were originally intended for business people on the road. But soon ordinary people were buying the phones for personal use. An abbreviation of Short Message Service, Matti

Makkonen pioneered SMS while working for Nokia Networks and Tele Finland. He pitched the concept of text messaging and helped to get the technology implemented in the 1990s.

GPS (SWE)

Remember the days of unfolding a large paper map and following a tiny line with your finger, trying to figure out if you were even on the right road, all while steering the car? Or maybe you had a co-driver who screamed directions at you and flipped out when you took a wrong turn?

Håkan Lans's Global Positioning System became the world standard for shipping and civil aviation. It is the basis for the GPS we use on our digital phones and everywhere else today.

CHRISTIANIA BIKE (DEN)

In 1984, Lars Engstrøm made a cargo bike as a present for his girlfriend. It was practical and stylish and attracted the local community to ask him to make some more. The tricycle, known as the Christiania bike, is not only the Danes' favourite, but can be found anywhere in the world. Because of its magnificent construction, it's used for transporting heavy things and is ideal for families and friends who want to share a bike ride.

LAZYTOWN (ISL)

Magnús Scheving published a children's book called LazyTown in 1991. The book centred around superhero Sportacus, who tried to teach the inactive inhabitants of LazyTown about athletics. Scheving commissioned his idea to Nickelodeon in 2003. He wanted to fight for a healthier lifestyle among children. LazyTown the TV series ran for three seasons and aired in over, 180 countries.

National identity of the Countries

While the Nordics are, of course, more than just an emblem, the national flowers, animals and symbols of the Nordic countries have a rich history. Here's a quick reference guide to the symbols you may encounter when learning about the Nordics.

Sweden

National Personification: The strong female warrior or Valkyrie, is also known as shieldmaiden is Sweden's iconic symbol. She holds a shield in front of her and stands beside a lion. The name of the lady is Svea and she represents the national identity of Sweden. You also have the coat of arms with three crowns (tree kronor) that you see used when talking about symbols of Sweden.

National Animal: Elk

National Flower: Small bluebell

Finland

National Personification: The Finnish Maiden is the symbol of Finland. She is called Aura and is described and has braided blonde hair, blue eyes, wearing a blue and white national costume or a white dress.

As a symbol, the Finnish Maiden has been used since the 19th century when she was pictured as a woman wearing a crown. The Finnish Maiden became younger as Finland gained a national consciousness and independence. Lion with a crown is in the Finland's coat of arms holding sword while trampling a sabre and used as a national symbol.

National Animal: Brown bear and whooper swan

National Flower: Lily-of-the valley

Norway

National Personification: Ola Nordmann is a national personification of Norwegians. The female counterpart is Kari Nordmann. Kari and Ola Nordmann are used to describe the stereotypical Norwegian family or household.

National Animal: Lion (royal national animal), white-throated dipper (national bird), fjord horse (national animal)

National Flower: Sedum and heather

Denmark

National Personification: Ogier the Dane became more widely known as Holger Danske, and was given the pedigree of being Olaf, son of King Gøtrik in the 16th century. Since then, Holger Danske has become a Danish folklore hero and eventually a symbol of Danish identity and patriotism.

National Animal: Red squirrel (national mammal), mute swan (national bird), small tortoiseshell (national butterfly)

National Flower: Daisy

Iceland

National Personification: The Lady of the Mountain (fjallkonan) is the national personification of Iceland. Lady of the Mountain is shown with a crown, fire erupting from it, and Iceland's most characteristic bird, the black raven on her shoulder.

National Flower: White dryad

National Animal: Gyrfalcon

LEFT: *Lily of the valley*

Nordic Mythology

Every country has their own folk stories. You might have heard about the Viking gods Thor, Freyr and Freyja. You are less likely to have come across Ukko Ylijumala or Väinämöinen.

The Finnish national epic is 19th century poetry compiled by Elias Lönnrot who travelled in Karelia and Finland recording the oral folklore and mythology and publishing the book *Kalevala*, as it is known today. Kalevala begins with the traditional Finnish creation myth, leading into stories of the creation of the earth, plants, creatures, and the sky.

Interestingly, Sweden does not have a national epic like the Finns. Their saga was written down by the Icelanders as it was already forgotten in Sweden. Iceland's *Njáls saga* is the longest and most highly developed of the Nordic sagas.

Most of the other countries have folklores that are based on common mythological creatures that you would have heard about before.

Mythical creatures of the North
TROLL/TROLDE

Trolls are several types of human-like supernatural beings in Scandinavian folklore. They are mentioned in the Edda old Icelandic literary works (1220) as a monster with many heads. You find trolls as characters in fairy tales, stories and songs.

Trolls are mostly described as slow, stupid and confused. In fairy tales, the troll is usually the evil but dumb opposition that humans conquer. Trolls come in many different shapes and forms. They are believed to live in the mountains, under the bridge or on the lake. Mountain trolls are described as rich with gold as detailed in Ibsen's *Peer Gynt*.

HULDRA

Huldra is known as a seductive forest creature or nymph. She is called the 'forest spirit', 'pine tree Mary' or Tallemaja in Swedish folklore. Saami folklore calls her Ulda and in Iceland Huldufólk. Huldra spirits are known to behave and look like humans. They are mischievous yet protective of humans.

NISSE/TOMPTE/TONTTU

These small creatures are generally described as being short with a long white beard. They wear conical red knitted caps and look like garden gnomes.

Nisse are thought to live in houses, saunas or barns. They are secret guardians of the homestead. They protect the family and animals, but if treated badly they will bring misfortune to the family and lifestyle. They have short tempers when offended, and will play tricks, steal items or even kill animals.

The Finnish saunatonttu exists to make sure everyone behaves properly in the sauna. *Joulutonttu* (Christmas elves) are Father Christmas's helpers, but are similar to nisse in appearance.

ELVES

Elves were mainly beautiful female figures who lived in the woods, by the lake or in mounds of stones. Elves were seen dancing on misty mornings and performing elf magic in the forest.

If humans saw elves dancing, they were lured to think only a few moments had passed when really it was hours.

In folk stories, elves often play the role of disease spirits too. In order to protect their homes and livestock against elves, people would carve an elf cross (like a pentagram) onto buildings.

HALTIJA

This word means owner, lord master or bearer depending on the context. There are many different kinds of haltijas. There is *hyvä haltija* who is there to make your dreams come true and protect you from bad things.

The forest has its own *haltija*, the leader of which is *Tapio*, the king of the forest. It also means magical powers of the forest.

The water is covered with *haltija* as well. Their leader is *Ahti*, the king of the sea. *Veden v*äki (water folk) also refers to the magical power of water that can make people sick or heal them.

Haltija were seen as the basis of elves in J.R.R. Tolkien's fantasy trilogy *The Lord of the Rings*. He has taken lots of influence from the Nordic mythology and language as you may have noticed.

Nordic identity is displayed through symbols of mythology and we come together through culture and sports, but you might wonder what Nordic lifestyle actually entails. That is what we are going to discover next.

EXPLORER 16ᵀᵀ

PART FOUR

LIVE LIKE THE NORDICS

What is Nordic Lifestyle?

What does it mean to live a Nordic lifestyle? That's the question we'll be answering in this chapter as we discover what Nordic lifestyle looks like up close, what you can take from the Nordic way of living and how you can implement it in your life to make it simpler, slower and more sustainable.

The Nordic countries are known for their beautiful nature, the Northern Lights, the landscape that you look at longingly wishing you were able to travel there. I do not blame you. Having grown up in rural Finland, there is nothing more exciting to me than being able to walk freely in the forest.

Walking in the forest is everyman's right, *allemansrätten*. In the Nordic countries, everyone by law is allowed to ramble for their leisure and enjoy the peace and quiet. Go eat fresh berries from the woods, fish from still waters, forage mushrooms for your meal, pick flowers...

This is the essence of what Nordic lifestyle means.

Outdoorsy lifestyle

Perhaps one of the reasons why the Nordic people love outdoor pursuits, or friluftsliv as the Norwegians like to call it, is because of nature and the connection we feel towards it. People have had to earn their living from the land since before the Viking times. The unforgiving terrain and harsh climate meant that you needed strong unwavering people to live in this part of the world.

After all, Nordic weather is unforgiving, but people still go out and enjoy the fresh air.

OPENING SPREAD: *Nuuksio, Finland*
NEXT SPREAD: *Foraging*

There is no bad weather just inadequate clothing.
Nordic saying

Sports that kids grow up with – like skiing, skating and ice hockey – are core physical activities at school. People are raised to be active from childhood, hence exercise is part of the Nordic psyche.

Even older people in Nordic countries tend to walk more from place to place than perhaps in Australia where people take the car for even short distances. Groups go Nordic pole walking together, as well as roaming and foraging in the forests. The older generation is more connected with nature than perhaps the current generation who lovs to live in the digital world.

Like in many other countries around the world, even younger Nordic people have become disconnected from nature and overly urbanised, often avoiding strenuous activity. Being more active and taking care of my body is my antidote for this trend towards a lack of movement.

Connection with nature

People in the Nordics enjoy nature. They value it. They have a connection to nature in a way many people elsewhere don't. Yet having greenery, trees and grass around you de-stresses you.
Having nature nearby is calming hence why the cities in the Nordics are surrounded by parks, forests and water. Look to any of the capital cities in the Nordics and there is plenty of water, sea and parks around. We are connected to nature from birth and it is enforced in the way we live our everyday lives.

In order to feel nature around you, perhaps you could bring some plants or flowers inside? There are studies saying that people are more centred and less stressed when they look after plants.

HAPPY HEALTHY DIET

A happy diet does not mean binge-eating to your heart's content. It means enjoying the food you eat, taking time to eat,

spending time at the dinner table with the family, having portion control... Not too much, not too little, just enough. Lagom like the Swedes say.

Think about the food when you're eating it and savour the taste. Don't rush or focus on the next thing you have to do. Take a moment to enjoy the meal and food that you are eating.

Like Italians, we Nordics love to sit around the table and have a nice meal with the family. With Finns, it might not be full of chatter, more so quiet moments with some occasional conversation. A friend described the experience like going to church. Eating dinner with family in the Nordics can be a precious moment. Savour and enjoy.

All in moderation

The Nordic people try not to indulge in things. They enjoy what they have, what they do. All in moderation means that you need to moderate your behaviour to enjoy life a little bit more.

Sounds easy, right? Yet behaviour change is not easy. When you are used to finishing a meal, it can be hard to stop halfway through when you are full. I know I've been there.

Indulging means consuming food, drink, shopping or whatever it is you think you need to look and feel complete inside of yourself. Instead of overindulging, enjoy a little food, a drink or enjoy the new pair of jeans you bought.

Enjoy life more

Living like the Nordics is about enjoying life instead of being in this constant battle of doing something new and trying something different and just going from one thing to another. When we live like this, we don't stop! We just go, go, go.

This is what the Nordics do so well. Like having a *fika,* we enjoy life and value every moment we can. Enjoying life *could* be learning something new or travelling to places you have never visited. However, it could be reading a book or baking. Look at what you already have and how you can enjoy that more.

Reduce stress

All these things I've been talking about so far in this chapter are about reducing stress. Enjoying life, taking everything in moderation, having a happy diet and surrounding yourself with nature, they all reduce stress. But what else can you do to reduce your stress levels?

In the Nordics, the number one way to de-stress would be having a sauna. Sauna is common in many households in the Nordics. For you, it might be having a massage, going to a spa to relax, listening to music or reading. You might like sitting by the sea, watching the waves and just letting time go by. Whatever it is that you do to unwind, do more of it.

Have sisu

Sisu is what we all carry inside of ourselves. Sisu is not a thing that you can buy. It is about how we express our character and get through when times are hard. During the global pandemic, this is what got us through: sisu.

Silence

In *Sisu: The Finnish Art of Courage*, Joanny Nylund talks about silence. Silence is part of who we are and where we come from. We do not find silence depressing or embarrassing. We are comfortable with silence, whether around people or in the forest.

> *"Finns view silence as a resource,*
> *not an embarrassment."*
>
> Joanna Nylund

I find it easy to be quiet when conversation drops off around me. I am comfortable just talking when I have something to say and being quiet when I have nothing to say. I can do small talk when I have to, but most of the time I am comfortable being an observer of the conversation.

However, many Finns nowadays have happy chatter, can do small talk and are more equipped to converse and get to know people than perhaps a few generations ago.

Mindfulness

I find it easy to relax. This was not always the case. It's about getting into the right state of mind, which can happen when I'm alone with myself or surrounded by nature. When you sit and really observe your surroundings, you find there is so much to be grateful for and a peace in which you cannot but forget your worries and your busy life.

The way we Finns relax by using nature and sauna as an antidepressant is great. Can you just walk in the forest and forget your worries? The Finns think you can. I, for one, can easily just take my dog and go for a walk without having to think about anything but where I am going and the next step.

Another way of relaxing and getting your mind to switch off is, of course, the sauna. Sitting in the sauna and letting your worries melt away, busy-ness is left at the door. You just sit and allow your mind to wander. There is no better place to do business or political deals, or you can just natter about the day in general. When you are free from of your clothes, you are free of inhibitions. You bear your soul to the world and the people around you.

 # Sustainable Nordics

Most of us are taught how to behave, to say 'please' and 'thank you', but how many of us know what we can recycle and what we cannot? Do we teach our children such skills at home or at school?

Maybe in your country they do teach sustainability, but in so many countries they don't. Although there are lots more emphasis on environmental actions these days, it is not enough. We need to make sure children follow our example and we need to set a good example for them.

Sustainable life starts at home and is the basis of Nordic life. In this chapter, I'm going to tell you what you can do to help yourself and your family live more of the sustainable concepts of the Nordics.

How Nordic countries led the sustainability movement

In the Nordic countries, there is a clear history of innovation, recycling and 'using what you have' principles. The Nordic countries are known for experimenting with sustainable technology, as we have a curiosity for life and how we can use things more efficiently. Many times, Nordic people have attempted new ways that probably didn't work out, but through innovation and persistence, they created technology that worked to make a difference.

One example is the great inventions in geothermal heating and how this has become mainstream. Using geothermal underfloor heating systems is common in today's Nordic countries. This technology was in its infancy 20 years ago but advancements in technology have allowed houses to be more self-sufficient using this kind of energy. Even old houses can move across to geothermal energy and embrace a more sustainable carbon footprint.

Many of my friends in Australia have wanted to switch to more renewable energy sources. Here, we would do that by using solar panels, but in the colder Nordic climate, wind power and geothermal are more efficient.

Greta Thunberg

Swedish climate activist Greta Thunberg has spoken about countries not doing enough to cut carbon emissions in the new digital era. Her vision has inspired millions around the world to make a change. Cutting plastic use, reducing carbon emissions and limiting flights are some initiatives that Greta has started. She has shown that one school girl from Sweden can make a big difference in the world. We all can make a difference.

Greta has said she will continue her climate protest in front of the Swedish Parliament until the Swedish government meets her demands. She is requesting that the country adheres to the carbon emissions target agreed by world leaders in Paris 2015. Are her demands too ambitious? Would she achieve more by working with the Swedish government? Interestingly, when you ask the Swedish government to comment about her request on the carbon emissions target, the answer is 'no comment.'

Nordic sustainability

In Nordic countries, everything is recycled. Look at Sweden. They bring in waste from other countries so that they can keep their recycling plants going... That's how efficient they are at recycling! Recycling is a core concept of Nordic living. It's been made so easy for people to recycle, as there are recycling points in shopping centres and shops everywhere.

Everything from batteries to medications to bottles to plastic bags can be recycled. This could so easily be introduced in other countries. Unfortunately, the governments in many countries have different priorities. This might be the case where you live as well. Lydia Lassila, Australian Olympic freestyle skier, talked to me

about this on The Nordic Mum podcast saying that it makes her angry and sad that something that could be so easily implemented in Australia but has been stalled by government inaction.

Thankfully, there are signs of change. We can all make change happen by demanding action from our members of parliament. At a grassroots level, we can start small – with ourselves. Recycle what you have - bottles, plastic, paper. Where can you recycle? How can you recycle? Ask these questions in your community and start putting recycling at the forefront of people's minds.

Growing things

When I interviewed author Jesse Karjalainen on my podcast about seven interesting facts about Sweden, he told me how Swedes are embracing the eco-friendly life. And it's not just about Swedes' love for the environmental movement and sustainability. This is about people actually caring about where their food is grown, how it gets to the shops and how it is packaged.

Over in Finland where people are looking into meat alternatives, you will now find things on supermarket shelves that are made from plants that look like meat. If you are vegan or vegetarian today, it's so much easier than it was even a few years ago to find meat alternatives. You can find meat made of pulled oats, as well as beef alternatives like *härkäpapumurska* made from Nordic fava beans. There are milk protein alternatives called *Mifu* and a Swedish bean-based meat alternative *Oumph*. Traditional sausage-makers have started to add meat-free sausages to their product ranges. You could call this a vegetarian revolution.

Nordics want to be at the front of sustainable change. The subject is well-researched and taught in schools. If you take just one lesson from this book, it is that you can be a Greta Thunberg and start making change wherever you are.

Perhaps sitting every Friday on government steps is not your thing but you could try starting conversations with your local parliamentary representatives or getting involved in your community to make sure sustainable changes are implemented.

Start with simple things like recycling whatever you can where you are. Begin by asking the member of parliament for your area for more recycling points. Initiate a collection of glass bottles with your neighbours and take them to recycling bins if they are not located near where you live. Establish an environmental movement calling for action and becoming an activist.

Even imperfect actions count if we all make these choices. I do not want to preach about the environment and a plastic-free life, but the Nordics have set the bar high and other cultures can aim just as high by voting for change.

Next I am going to talk about sauna and why it is such an integral part of Nordic culture. Yes, you find saunas in all the Nordic countries but not perhaps in the way you imagine.

 **Sauna**

You cannot visit the Nordics without knowing about sauna. The word 'sauna' travelled from Byzantium through Slavik culture to the Nordics. One of the first written descriptions of the Finnish sauna was in 1112.

Monk and historian Nestor the Chronicle described it as "hot wooden saunas in which naked bathers beat themselves with branches and pour cold water over themselves". Sounds like the modern sauna in today's Finland.

Sauna history

We can trace the history of sauna back to the Bronze Age in the 1500s where the first saunas were dug as holes in the ground in a hut. People would warm them up with stones placed underneath and the smoke would travel up through holes in the slats. The smoke sauna would be topped with a notch, a kind of tarpaulin, and there you have a traditional smoke sauna.

Later, saunas were built above ground with wooden logs. The rocks were heated in a stone stove with a wood fire. This room did not have a chimney but a small air vent on the back wall. Smoke would fill the room while it was heating. Once the rocks were hot throughout, it was ready to use. This sauna was called *savu* (Finnish for smoke) sauna.

From the 1600s, we find the Finns' love of sauna mentioned by historians who had travelled there. We can find further mention of sauna in 1799, when Italian explorer Giuseppe Acerbi travelled to Finland. He described a detailed encounter with Finns having high temperature saunas. There would have been birch tree sticks involved, where you beat yourself red while soaking in the heat of the sauna.

Sauna today

Today's sauna is almost a spiritual place for Finns. There are over 3 million saunas in Finland against 5 million people living there. Sauna is a place to cleanse yourself before you take a bath or shower in ice cold water.

Throughout the times, sauna has been used to prepare food and for giving birth. When access to medical care was sparse, the sauna was the cleanest place to deliver babies. I still recall my grandmother's friend telling me that her parents were born in the sauna, so this was only a few generations ago.

People with illnesses were treated there as well, including by cupping with cow horns, where you bled in the heat. Sauna was also used to smoke meat and fish.

Medical benefits of bathing in sauna

Research shows frequent sauna bathing is associated with a reduced risk of cardiac disease, inflammation and high blood pressure. We also know sauna relieves symptoms of the common cold. People use sauna as a place to relax and reflect. Athletes use it to remove lactic acid from their system. It is a place of relaxation for muscles after exercise or high performance sport. The relaxing benefits of sauna have made it a must-have in a Nordic home.

You can find sauna in most homes and corporations. Even Burger King in Finland has a sauna, as does Parliament House in Helsinki. Legend says they have made many political deals sweating on the seats of the Parliament House sauna.

Jos ei sauna terva ja viina auta, on tauti kuolemaksi.
Old Finnish proverb meaning: if liquor, tar and sauna
won't help, an illness is fatal.

What is the difference between bastu and sauna?

Do other Nordic countries enjoy sauna like the Finns? Yes, they do. *Bastu* or *badstu* are commonplace in all the Nordic countries. In other Nordics, though, it is more usual to see them in hotels, spas, swimming pools and wellness centres, and not so common in residential houses except in Sweden and Finland. For example, in Iceland, they have far more hot springs, pools and geothermal pools than saunas.

The obsession with sauna prompted the World Sauna Championships, where the winners have been mostly Finns. However, they have not arranged the Championship since 1990 when a contestant from Russia died after spending six minutes at 110°C. The winner that year, a Finn, had burns as well and required medical attention.

Etiquette

If they invite you for a sauna night in Finland, it includes some sort of food, barbeque in summer and drinks as well as having a sauna. You might go all together or ladies together and men together. You are expected to be nude. Yes, nude.

If you feel embarrassed, wrap a towel around you. Take all your jewellery off, because metal feels hot against the skin in the hot steam. There should be a sauna mat that you can sit on. Remember to not lean on the wall, as it can burn you. With all these warnings in mind, enjoy the relaxing hot steam around you. Finns are quiet in the sauna; you can talk but you may find people are more comfortable just sitting and relaxing without the need to chat.

Remember to ask if you are going to add more water. As sauna etiquette, you want to make sure people are comfortable for you to increase the temperature. Anything between 40-60°C is tolerable. When you have had enough, say so. Once you are ready, make your way to cool down, swim in an icy lake or have a shower. Or just sit outside enjoying the cold with a beer in hand. Sauna reflects the Nordic culture of taking life slow, relaxing and spending time with your friends and family. Sauna is an egalitarian place. There are no titles or hierarchies there.

I still remember when my British boyfriend came to Finland and was asked to go for a sauna for the first time. He did not know what to do, as it was a mixed sauna. I think he hoped to be swallowed up by the floor and pretended to be interested in the hot rocks to the point he nearly burned his head.

Finns are more comfortable with nudity than our Nordic neighbours, at least for sauna. For anything else, no, but for sauna, it comes easily to us, as we are not shy about taking off our clothes.

Next, we'll indulge in some Nordic design and Nordic minimalism, as well as how you can include these as part of your everyday life.

Nordic Design

When describing Nordic design, my first thoughts are about the clean, clean lines, practical objects, hints of colour, textures like natural wood in different shades and fabrics that complement the space. How Nordic people use design in their everyday life is by making it useful and practical.

I have spoken to many designers about what attracts them to Nordic design. The answer is always practicality and being easy on the eye. When reflecting on the main pillars of Nordic design from those conversations, I came up with this;

- **Simplicity** – the logical solution refined to the point of removing anything unnecessary
- **Functional** –practical for the user and the right proportions
- **Sustainability** –timeless and built to stand the test of time

When we look at brands like Marimekko, Artek and Fritz Hansen, what they have in common is that they have been able to evolve over time. How these brands have lasted strongly relates to what has happened in history, especially the end of World War Two. At that time, there was support from the Nordic governments to grow these industries. Furniture makers were encouraged to use local manufacturing, furniture design and materials from their countries, such as birch in Finnish design. This helped kickstart exports of these products and Nordic design was exported along with it.

Many of these companies have had to to make changes to how they present themselves. For example, Marimekko and Royal Copenhagen have employed new designers who think innovatively. Collaborations with other brands like Marimekko with Adidas and IKEA with several up-and-coming designers have made them popular with a new generation of fans.

Nordic brands last longer

Another reason these brands have lasted is that Nordic design is very affordable and accessible for everyone. This is another aspect of the Nordic way of living. Everyone has a piece of Scandinavian furniture or tableware in their homes. The amount of Ittala, Arabia or Marimekko we have managed to hoard over the years in our house is quite astonishing. And we have not even lived together in Finland as a family. We have bought or been given lots of presents of this kind. Nordic people living abroad often have those nostalgic pieces to remind them of home.

Earlier, I talked about IKEA and its global domination in how it applies its functional, practical design. However, IKEA furniture is mass-produced and sustainability is not one of the core values that you would associate with the company. People often buy IKEA furniture thinking that they will get rid of it when they can. There are calls for a war on IKEA wastage with the aim of making their products more sustainable. In council clean-ups, 40% of furniture waste is from IKEA. Since the company has a large market, it needs to create home design and quality that is more sustainable.

Change is coming to IKEA stores, though, with solar panels on IKEA warehouses, a used items return policy and more sustainable, durable furniture which it is working on over time. I no longer have it on my conscience if I buy from IKEA!

We are Shivria, we are Oxes, we will not give up,
we will find a way.
Ingvar Kamprad, founder of IKEA

Repurposing and recycling

Here in Australia, repurposing and recycling of furniture is still very rare and difficult. Nordic countries are so much further ahead on this and there is lots being done to make it even easier.

The purpose of our home is to have connection with ourselves, our family and with nature. Our homes provide this to us. If we look after our homes and nurture ourselves, we can go and look after the world.

If you want to have more Nordic feel to your home, there are few ideas you can implement right away:

- Take away the down-lights and put some nice up-lighting in your space, perhaps a lamp on a stand in the corner
- Light some candles and put on the coffee
- Move the furniture away from the corners of the room so that you can interact with people more easily
- Have a few statement pieces around the home, quality designs that light up the place

When I look at my house, I always remember the interview I did with Nicola Capper, a blogger and Nordic design enthusiast, and what she said about the look and feel of Nordic design.

"It's very much about the light. It's about the natural elements, and choosing well, and the craftsmanship and the quality of what you're buying rather than the quantity."

Nicola Capper

The future of Nordic Design

There is a lot to be said about Nordic design and how innovative it will be going forward into the next decade and beyond. Sustainability will play a bigger part in the design process, usage and overall purpose of any item. Handicraftsman, who produce quality pieces will have more of a place in production of furniture in the future, I think, as the consumerism we have become accustomed to will have to stop even in the Nordics. The power that the consumer has is to vote with their wallet, will be stronger than ever before, when there are more sustainable options.

I hope that Nordic design will take the lead, inspire and develop more sustainable products and stay true to its Nordic heritage while setting an example for other brands to follow.

When we look at the Nordic design, we see a very minimalistic flavour, but what is Nordic minimalism as a lifestyle? That's coming up next in the following chapter.

Minimalism the Nordic Way

When I talk about Nordic minimalism, I talk about it as a holistic lifestyle not just about the décor. Nordic minimalism is about owning fewer possessions and a 'less is more' approach in life, enjoying what you have and living a life of moderation.

I come from a family in Finland where my mother was the original frugal mum. She taught us that we did not need the newest of the new for everything out there. My mother would tell us we could fix things that were broken rather than have a new one. She taught us to value what we have, how to mend something when it is broken, and recycle or upcycle wherever we can.

I remember feeling embarrassed in the shops when she was getting a many-times-used plastic bag out of her handbag and putting the shopping in there - something that is quite normal now. At the time, it felt like she was being too tight with money. Why couldn't she buy a new shiny plastic bag like everybody else's mum? But she did not. She was saving the planet one plastic bag at a time! I just did not see it like that back then.

Something else I remember my mother doing was using baking paper again and again. When we made cinnamon buns, she would carefully remove the buns from the baking paper and store it in a drawer for another use. Just like with the plastic bags, she was thinking: *why waste it when you can use it again?*

Now I have adopted my mother's approach: minimising waste and recycling what we have.

Nordic minimalistic living is actually about having *more* – more *life* – but what does that even mean? Having more life is about enjoying a walk by the beach with water washing the shores and listening to the birds sing. It's the crisp noise that snow makes under your shoes on a cold winter's day. Enjoying those

moments without having to look at the clock, without having to think about what happens next, where you have to be or what you need to do. And especially not: *have I posted an Insta picture about this moment?*

This chapter explores some of the ways we can do that. So let's start here – with what distracts us the most...

Getting off technology

Nordic minimalism stretches all the way to the mind as well, and it not just about our physical surroundings. When I removed distractions like social media apps from my life, I started seeing the way it is meant to be lived.

How often do we look at our phone just to see how many times someone has liked our picture? How often do we pick up our phone automatically when we should be looking at our children playing or having a conversation? Phones have become a distraction.

Social media is about connecting people and making it easier to keep up to date with your relatives in faraway countries. We must consider when we need to *live* - not through our screen but by looking at what is around us. We need to create more space.

To do this, I went on a cleaning spree on my phone and deleted lots of things I did not need or even know I had. I took back control of my life by removing and limiting the information overload I was experiencing.

Minimalism is about having less to worry about as well. I challenge you to remove your social media apps for a day and see how you feel. I bet you feel lost for while. Like, what are you supposed to do with your hands, with your time?

Nordic minimalism is being intentional with your actions to be able to focus more on what matters, buy less, consume less and have a better quality to your life. It also gives your mind the freedom to wander, to processing emotions, and to think about things that you perhaps didn't even know needed attention.

Living the minimalist life

Nordic minimalist life is about being connected to nature, walking bare-footed and taking time to reflect. It is about eating fresh produce, baking and cooking from scratch, taking steps to recycle, repair, reuse and repurpose. Sounds wonderful, right? Yet becoming minimalist is hard. I'm not going to lie. It is difficult. You need to have the right mindset to get started. When I say that sustainability and minimalism is part of Nordic lifestyle, Nordic people have learned it over time. We are taught by our parents and it becomes part of who we are as Nordic people. If you want to start a more minimalist Nordic lifestyle, it can be tough to implement because of what you have to let go.

One time, I was asked, "How does your husband take on minimalist thinking and the minimalist approach?" He is kind of okay with it, but sometimes just does not get the changes I want to implement. His brain resists rewiring and adapting to accept new ways of living. You can embrace minimalism many ways. I recommend starting with one change you want to make. Once that improvement is implemented and it becomes part of your life, move on to another one.

If you do not enjoy having a minimalist approach, then perhaps it is not for you. Maybe you need to look at some other aspects of your life to change those instead. Enjoy what you are doing. Embrace one aspect first. Let it ripple through other parts of your life.

- Get your mindset right
- Look at your house and how you want to live your life
- Get rid of items that are not needed using the Swedish death cleaning döstädning concept for assessing what you want to keep and what you want to get rid of before you die
- Recycle, reuse, repurpose and repair

Minimalism does not need to be boring. Minimalism is about having a purpose for the things in our lives as we realise we don't need everything we have. We can live with less clutter and have more purpose to do things that we enjoy.

Nordic people are the ultimate minimalists with their lives. They live like minimalists and they do not even know it! Society and culture are simply geared towards maximising enjoyment without maximising *stuff*.

Nordic minimalism in your home

If you look at a Nordic house, you will see that every piece of furniture has its purpose and place. The house is clean, not crowded, practical but not sparse. Many of the pieces are practical, durable, made to be appreciated for a long time and built to last. Marimekko, Iittala, IKEA, Kosta Bode are just a few of the names you might see.

There are also brands like Svensk Tenn that have sustainability as one of their core values. And you know those IKEA chairs that were bought 20 years ago? They are still in use in use today as they were made to last. Nordic minimalism is all about simplicity, purity and calm. It is about buying less and buying better.

In furniture, this often means wood, where sustainable options are available. Colours may be greys and pastels. Design is sleek and clean. Imagine a summer cottage by the lake...the small, practical cottage that is comfortable and radiates with hygge. These are the pictures that come to mind when thinking about Nordic minimalism.

Nordic design is a product of its environment. Harsh conditions have forced people to evolve, innovate and be practical about design. And you too can have this kind of Nordic minimalism in your home and it starts with a mindset.

"Buy quality, buying little, with each object having a
practical place in everyday life."
Susanna Heiskanen, The Nordic Mum

How can you have more quality time in your life when you own less stuff? What do I mean when I say this? The pastime of foraging is a good example. When you go into nature, you take care of it. In Finland, we pick berries. In Sweden, it might be mushrooms. We only take what we need and always leave enough for the animals in the forest because we live in symbiosis with them. Nature gives us what we *need*, not what we *want*.

> *"The purest joys in life come from being grateful and showing it to the world."*
> Susanna Heiskanen, The Nordic Mum

When you apply this method to your life, you start looking at the space that you live in. Do you have too much stuff? Do you need all these things? Could you survive with less? Yes, you can survive with less! Do not store stuff! Be firm on what you do and do not need.

Clearing the area around you creates space in your life and mind because there are fewer things to clean, store or maintain. You will be amazed by how much you can get rid of if you ask yourself whether you need or want it. Avoid creating emotional attachments to items or being overly sentimental. Let go of things when they are no longer needed.

Kitchen makeover

I need to talk about the minimalist kitchen because we spend so much time in this room. The kitchen is the soul of a home, I believe. We all love the kitchen. We also need to spend some time in our kitchens, even if we are not fond of cooking. So if you want to start a minimalist journey, the kitchen is a great place to begin.

These tips will give you a great starting point wherever you are.

Roughly one-third of the food produced in the world for human consumption every year — approximately 1.3 billion tonnes — gets lost or wasted. When we create less waste and use more of what we have, freeze food (such as milk, tomatoes), dry food (such as herbs, mushrooms, berries), we all are better off. Think about the following in your own home:

- Can you have a compost in the back of your garden to make mulch?
- Can you buy food in bulk?
- Are there local products or a co-op that you can use?
- Can you avoid using plastic kitchen wrap or find biodegradable or sustainable alternatives?
- Can you grow your own produce in communal gardens, your own back yard, or even on your balcony?
- Can you cook what you have, rather than desiring more and more produce and ending up with food in the bin?
- Can you plan your life so that you reduce waste and unnecessary expenditure, for example, by menu-planning?
- How can you incorporate as much seasonal produce on your menu as possible?
- Remove all clutter from your kitchen tops.
- Rearrange and get rid of unnecessary furniture from your kitchen.
- Use quality chopping boards, knives and plates that will last a long time.
- Have a few pieces of furniture and items that hold meaning for you.

Being grateful and intentional

It goes without saying that we should be grateful for what we have, but do we practice this? Are you intentionally giving thanks for your life and possessions? The Nordics have learned to enjoy life with less, having a more meaningful purpose for anything and everything.

In some ways, it is going to the sauna, spending time in nature, doing sports, taking in the quiet of the forest, enjoying that relaxing feeling at the end of the working week or clearing the negative thoughts from your mind.

Next let's explore hygge to understand how you can be intentionally happy and how enjoying the little things can spread contentment to other areas of your life.

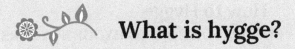

What is hygge?

Hygge is the Danish word for cosiness. Hygge is a state of mind. You don't need anything to have hygge. Hygge is everywhere. It is whatever you feel comfortable and cosy doing, whatever makes you happy.

A few years ago, happiness professor Meik Wiking started talking about this concept and published *A Little Book of Hygge*. And people went crazy for it! They still love it today. This book defined hygge as a word, but also how you can practice it. Several books have been written about the subject since.

A Little Book of Hygge book has become the pillar for many people who are looking for a slower life than what they have. I wonder if Meik Wiking knew he was creating a phenomenon when he wrote his book. Probably not to the extent it took off! Yet people wanted to simplify their life and this book was answer.

There are lots of misconceptions of what hygge is and how to have it. You don't need to *buy* anything to be happy or have hygge. You might even have to get rid of things more so than acquiring anything. There are items like soy candles, cushions and blankets sold under name of hygge. People are monetising this concept, which makes me slightly nauseated when I look at my social media feed. I often see people saying you need this or that to have hygge, but those people have misinterpreted the whole purpose of it.

✺ How to Hygge

SIX TIPS FOR HOW TO HYGGE BY YOURSELF

Here is my answer to applying hygge to your life. It's time to put some cosy slow living into your life and simplify things...

- ### Declutter your life starting with your home

  Let's start with your surroundings. How can you have a more meaningful existence with less stuff? Look at one room at a time and see how you can make it cosier.

  Make sure that the items you keep are practical and have a functional purpose. That is not to say you should not keep your grandmother's teacups. Sentimental items have their place. However, take a good look at what you need, what you want to repair, what to give to charity and what to recycle. Remember that you can use Facebook groups to buy, sell and exchange anything you want to get rid of that is no longer needed.

  No one is comfortable and cosy in a busy and crowded home. Once you have done your home, removing other unwanted items from your life becomes easier.

- ### Decluttering your mind

  I am a list person. It keeps me on track and makes me get things done. Perhaps you need reminders on your phone, Post-It notes or a list on the fridge to make things happen, but once you get in the habit of using one of these methods you will find that you are more on top of daily tasks and it becomes much easier to do as well.

  Having a list and also putting a journal next to your bedside table is a great idea. When you have ideas, thoughts or conversations that you want to get out of your head, just write them down. I get all my best ideas in the shower and have a pen there so that I can write on the wall when I come up with something.

  Decluttering the mind can be tricky and you may need some practice. Just closing your eyes, taking a deep breath, centring your thoughts and counting backwards will calm you and stop your mind drifting. It's like a mini yogi moment.

Part of decluttering your mind might be staying away from people who drain your energy and fill your mind with negativity, doubt and gossip. Yes, those who are pulling you down, those who have a negative influence and those who might want to use you for their own gain. You know who I'm talking about. We all have one of those people in our lives. This is why I say to declutter the mind first: you'll need to be firm and clear with yourself before you evaluate friendships, their meaning and whether they make you happy.

• Reading challenge

If you follow me on Instagram, you'll know that I read a lot. Every year I put a target on how many books I will read. My friend asked how I do it, when I have two kids. Where do I get the time? But reading ten pages every evening does not take that much time. You make time to do things that bring you happiness.

• Socialise more

When you have more time, you can go out more, see a movie, meet a friend and have a hyggelig time. Have a date night, host a dinner party, just be comfortable around your friends. Yes, having fewer digital devices equals more face-to-face interactions with people. There is so much hygge in this!

• Get walking

Whether it's Nordic walking, exercising or simply spending time outside, this is a wonderful way to have hygge.

I talk a lot about how Nordic people love outdoor life. Even in the harsh winter climate, they still go out. They love walking, skiing and all things to do with snow. No matter what the weather, we know how to enjoy it. We have become too stagnant in our modern lives. We can tend to say it is bad weather, too hot, too cold, too wet. Maybe we prefer to stay inside. But let's just dress for the occasion and the weather and get going.

Life is out there, not indoors!

SIX TIPS FOR HOW TO HYGGE AS A FAMILY

These were my pointers on how to hygge for yourself, but what about having hyggelig time with your family? What can you do to make the moment cosy with kids or grandkids? How do you keep the kids entertained, but keep them relaxed at the same time? It's tricky, I know, but I do have a few more tips on how to have stress-free hygge moments even if you have kids.

- **Spend time together as a family**

  This should be a no-brainer but then you start thinking what should we do? You could take that long walk, set up a movie night, play board games (like Monopoly) or cards. Kids just love spending time on these kinds of activities with you.

  A word of warning... Choose the activity carefully. At our house, Monopoly causes more issues and is not necessarily a relaxed activity!

- **Have book time**

  Having a hyggelig moment with your kids can be reading books to them or getting them to read books to you while you listen. In our family, we call it book time. Perhaps you have a comfortable book nook where you can curl up with them on cushions and read together.

- **How was your day?**

  Have a moment to connect before dinner asking how the day was for everyone. You could do this before or during dinner, but focus on paying attention to everyone by asking them a simple question so that they can offload any issues.

  This works like magic when you have kids who have a teenage attitude at age seven! Remember, if you do not ask, why should your kids ask you? Your behaviour sets an example to them.

- **Sit down for a family meal**
  Try to make that hyggelig moment a family meal together at least once a week. Perhaps you take everyone out for a weekly lunch or dinner. Have a picnic in the park with sandwiches or sit down at home and eat a home-cooked meal together. Kids love connecting with you at the table when you are all together.

- **Yoga to relax**
  My oldest surprised me when he asked to do yoga for the first time. He had seen my mat and obviously wanted to try it. We found this YouTube channel about kids' yoga and watched it together. We took the mats out and started doing yoga alongside each other. Every time the kids want to relax now, that is what happens. They do yoga and I try to join them, if it's not in the middle of cooking dinner.

- **Hot drink with pyjamas on**
  My favourite hyggelig moment with kids is drinking a hot drink in our PJs. Is there anything more comfortable than that? Kids love having their pyjamas on all day and so do us adults sometimes, so when it's cold or rainy outside, why not? Make a mulled wine for yourself, a hot chocolate or hot cranberry juice for your kids, and just hang out and have a hyggelig time with your little ones, warm drink in hand.

Time to start a new chapter on this life of self-discovery. Look for new good habits that you can embed in your life. Simplifying life is never easy but having less means more time to do what really brings you joy.

These chapters have given you some indication of how Nordics create happiness, but why are the Nordics such a happy place to live? That's what we're going to look at next.

PART FIVE

HOW NORDICS STAY HAPPY

Why the Nordic Countries have the happiest people in the world

With the long days of darkness, you may think the Nordic people are not a happy bunch. Well, incorrect! According to many surveys, local and global, the Nordics are a happy place to live.

Foreigners have difficulty understanding that Nordic people can be happy without smiling and verbalising their contentment. Happiness to us Nordics is something you cannot necessarily quantify. The World Happiness Report tries! It states that the little things like paying a compliment, opening a door and other small gestures are powerful ways to give and receive happiness.

"For instance, holding the door open for a stranger, paying someone a compliment, caring for a sick relative, comforting a spouse or returning a lost wallet are all small but meaningful forms of generous action."
World Happiness Report 2019

Based on questionnaire data, several reports have shown how happiness is rooted firmly in the Nordic corner of the world. Finland has been voted the happiest country for five years in a row by the World Happiness Report. The Danes are the happiest people according to European Social Survey. The rest of the Nordic countries top these kinds of surveys year on yemar.

Why are we so happy then?

"Finland is one of the countries that has the best environment and social systems to be happy. Finland has the great qualities that make people feel safe and a high standard of living, regardless of age, gender, or status."
Japanese expatriate living in Finland Daiki Yoshikawa

This is not to say that the Nordic countries are perfect. They have their fair share of socio-economical challenges. In fact, when living there, Nordic people do not tend to see how happy life really is. However, even with their own problems, being such peaceful and stable countries makes Finland and the rest of the Nordics a great place to live.

In Part Five, I am going to explore Nordic happiness and give you some answers on how you can create it for yourself wherever you are.

Happiness in the Nordics

They way Nordics live their life is admirable. When I was in Finland, I remember how nice it was to just be and enjoy the little things. Having a coffee and cake or gathering around the table and talking with loved ones, you do not need much more than that to be content and enjoy life.

What makes Nordic people happy? What are we talking about exactly when we talk about Nordic happiness? Is it all about living in the moment and loving life? When recording my podcasts, I have had to think about this many times. I have arrived at many different answers to the question 'What make Nordic people happy?' but I love what Ingrid Opstad, Norwegian blogger and writer, said the most.

"Find happiness in the small things."
Ingrid Opstad

Finland and happiness

Some people rave about the idea that Finland is where you find the happiest people on the planet. Finns shy away from this definition, as they don't feel it to be true. They point out that Finns do not smile and that Finland is cold and dark much of the year. Yes, these things are true, but what Finns have forgotten is that despite the gloomy light and low temperatures, at least the society, healthcare, education and government all still work, making Finland a safe place to live.

Happiness is not just about your bus coming on time. It is about feeling secure in your life, trusting the government and the system for running the country. The Global Happiness Report states that people who are more content with their life are more likely to spend money on and give gratitude for other people. These random acts of kindness are more likely to come from people who feel happy, trusting and safe. They will also increase the happiness that others around them feel about their life. When I talked about happiness in length on my 100th podcast episode, Japanese expatriate living in Finland, Daiki Yoshikawa, said:

"People in Finland don't tend to seek anything, especially happiness."

Daiki Yoshikawa

I would have to agree with him. Finns do not need to *do* anything to be happy. They are happy and grateful for what they have. It is a simple lifestyle with simple needs. That sums up the Finns and happiness to me.

Trust

One of the fundamental reasons why there is trust between people, society and government is that Finland has a well-functioning civil society. People do not need to worry about their basic welfare. They can go about their lives and live a stress-free existence. Varpu Rusila from Her Finland blog said that as a woman you can walk anywhere without fear.

"You can trust the people and you can trust the system. the news tells you the right news and not fake news. you can trust that the government is honest. and you can trust everyone surrounding you."

Varpu Rusila

Trust is one of the reasons why Finland is consistently ranked number one on the happiness surveys.

Freedom of choice

In Finland, there is universal healthcare, which means you get the same treatment and care no matter where you are. If you get sick, you go to the doctors. This is something to be happy about, yet Finns think this is such a normal thing. Once you

have lived overseas, you understand how lucky and privileged you are for living in Finland.

There is also freedom of choice that people take for granted. For years after I left Finland, I went back there to see my doctor and dentist. I just knew the care was better – and of course, free. Compared to systems like Australia and the US, where the care is only partially subsidised (or not at all), Finns have a lot to be thankful for when it comes to their wellbeing.

Education, freedom and lack of corruption

The education system is first class in Finland too. It is internationally recognised as one of the best, if not the best in the world. But Finns see it as having had too many changes, too many reforms, with overworked and unappreciated teachers. This might be the case. However, even with all of its faults, the Finnish education system is much better than many that other people put their kids through.

Finland has little or no corruption. There is also freedom of the press to challenge the government and policies that give freedom of expression without repercussions. People trust that their elected members of parliament will do their best to enhance their wellbeing and happiness.

All Nordic countries were in the top 10

And it's not just Finland. Yes, all the Nordic countries continue to make the top ten of the Global Happiness Report consistently year after year. Let's dive deeper into why happiness is so easily achieved in Denmark, Iceland, Sweden and Norway.

No wonder Danes are content with their hygge. They too have a stable society, as we can see from Denmark having the smallest wealth gap in the world. This is one of the main markers of social cohesion.

Iceland, with the most equality-driven society, was the first country in the world to enforce equal pay for women and men. More equality between the sexes brings harmony to the people and gives them less cause for disagreements.

Sweden has a high life expectancy and social support system, which lends itself to greater wellbeing and increased happiness too.

Is it any wonder why these countries are the envy of so many people who want to replicate the lifestyle in their own countries?

How can you have a piece of the Nordic lifestyle?

Recently, there has been a widespread upward trend in negative affect, comprising worry, sadness and anger in Asia and Africa. This negativity has been reflected in the US too and across the globe, showing these countries as less happy places to live.

"Social happiness is therefore even more relevant, in order to give a positive perspective and outlook for the present and for the future."

Andrea Illy, World Happiness Report

While we can't tackle global stress, sadness, anger and negativity as individuals, we have to start somewhere. On a micro scale, doing a random act of kindness, giving a stranger a compliment or spreading some goodwill can go a long way.

Start with the small things that you have control over, because individual happiness contributes to the happiness of your local area, which spreads to your whole country, and the world as a whole. Little by little, we have opportunities to spread some warmth.

How to create happiness in your life

Some of these healthy choices are guaranteed to make you happy. After all, we can't have happiness without health, can we?

EXERCISE

Nordic people have learned to fuel happiness with exercise. And it's entertaining too. They will go for a walk, a hike, go skiing, snowshoeing, ice-fishing, compete an obstacle course with their wife as a rucksack...there is clear correlation between exercise and happiness. Physical activity pumps up endorphins, the feel-good hormone credited for reducing stress levels.

FOOD

Ah, the goodness of a home-cooked meal. In the Nordics, we love to cook and bake. It is not uncommon to cook everything from scratch using what you can forage from the forest or pick from the garden. A home-cooked meal is an honour to eat when you go for a visit to someone's home.

I believe everything should be in moderation. Like the principle of *lagom,* it should be just right, not too much, not too little. We love to enjoy life but we need to make sure we get the right kind of fuel to do it and the right amount.

WALK BAREFOOT

The feeling of fresh grass underfoot...or sand. Or water. There is something really relaxing and uplifting about walking without shoes. I take off my shoes at the beach no matter what the weather.

Perhaps walking barefoot on snow is different! From the sauna to an ice hole, the sea or a lake perhaps, but nothing longer than that. The ice and snow can hurt, but it is refreshing as well.

MINDSET

When it is dark and cold, are you unhappy? No, say the Nordics. We always find things to do. Something to be happy about. Small things in life matter. If you think negative thoughts, you will talk negatively. But if you find simple things to enjoy, the opposite is true.

SAUNA

Relaxing and enjoying life without much small talk equals happiness to us Nordics. Just contemplate the view from the window and appreciate what you have.

# Parenting in Scandinavia

People in the Nordics love to raise their kids among nature from a young age. For little children, this translates to enjoying nature, playing, running, getting to know the animals, flowers and insects.

This gentle approach follows through to school-age kids who have lessons on the environment, biology and how to interact with nature.

Back in the days when I was in school in Finland, I would go as far as saying that we were taught what we can eat in nature. We used nettles for tea and ate sour-tasting grass leaves as snacks. We learned how to get ants' juice with a long stem of grass that you put into the nest. We discovered how to stop a bleed by pressing a certain leaf against a wound. These are a few examples of how kids are raised to respect and live with nature. Nordic parents teach their children to be independent from early on too. The root of this approach goes back to a time when there weren't schools in every village. You had to travel a long way by skis, bicycle or horse to get to your destination. Talk about survival and resilience! Nordic parenting has not changed that much from those days.

Something I find very different between Finland and Australia is our tolerance for dirt in the Nordics. We let kids get dirt on their hands, which is great for building immunity while they're young. Nordic parents are not afraid of germs and like to think that the more the kids are exposed to them in their childhood the better they are in the long run. As clean and tidy as we make our homes in the Nordics, we know that overcleaning increases the risk of some allergies and asthma.

In the Nordics, parents often think that children should be children as long as possible. It goes without saying that play is the best way to teach children life lessons. There is playtime in pre-schools in Finland that is the equivalent to kindy here in Australia. In Finland, playtime continues when school starts in year one, but in Australia play seems to be dropped by this time. I see a responsibility for parents to keep kids playing, making sure that they are interested in what is happening around them. This is the greatest gift we can give our children.

One day, my son asked me why we put green waste in the compost. This is what I mean by keeping kids interested in their environment, teaching them how to use what we have and not creating more waste than necessary. Showing the kids that we can live with nature and give back what we take. The recent talks about plastic pollution have made me question how many wipes and disposable nappies I used with my two kids. Would I do things differently now? With knowledge comes the responsibility to change. Yes, I am sure I would make some changes to my decisions. I can only look back with remorse and hope that the mothers after me will be better informed. And that knowledge I share will make a difference.

What can you learn from Nordic parents? Patience, taking small steps and learning from our mistakes. Take an interest in the world around you and notice nature. Get your kids excited about a sustainable life, help them recycle and trust your kids to learn from you.

What about education?

Finnish schools are based on the principle that children need to come first. Children start school the year they turn seven and have compulsory pre-school few hours a day year before that. The school days are short. Kids start at 9:00 am and are usually finished by 1:00 or 2:00 pm. The hours increase every year and the children are given homework but this is not excessive.

Schools are known to be supportive of kids on their learning path. There are no standardised tests and teachers are relied upon to teach the curriculum as they see fit. Success of schools in Finland is based on everyone being equal. All kids have the opportunity to succeed in life and are given the same start in education as the neighbour's kids.

How Finland mastered Pisa

Pisa testing is conducted annually to rank countries on how well they are doing. Finland has been top of the rankings for years. When I asked my sister Johanna about this, she said, *"Finnish teacher education is one of the best and most demanding in the world. To even become a classroom teacher, you need to have a master's degree in the field of education."* Johanna is an English teacher in primary school in Finland herself.

Teachers are trusted and have autonomy over their teaching. Of course, the national curriculum and syllabus create guidelines. Education is also valued in society and best of all it is free. The government put a lot of effort to create equal opportunities for all pupils all over Finland, though there is not much diversity among Finnish schools.

Like with any system, of course, there are issues in Finnish education. Teachers are leaving the profession due to burnout. There is a lack of funding for education and, in the digital age, device usage is causing problems with kids' behaviour. These issues cannot be corrected by the teachers alone. Johanna told me, *"Funding is becoming a problem. The municipalities organising education are lacking funds. We don't have enough people working and paying taxes. This is going to be a problem in the future as*

Finland is greying. The motivation of pupils is not always the best. The gap between those pupils who are doing well and those who are performing poorly is widening."

Digital devices

There has been lots of talk about digital devices and how they are impacting our children, what are kids doing with them at school and how we as parents should be parenting. When asked about devices, Johanna said, *"Schools must provide devices for the pupils needed in studying. You can use your own devices if parents give permission."*

Friluftsliv with kids

I suppose kids live friluftsliv as soon as they are out of the womb. They nap outside in the pram and spend time on the ground no matter what the weather wearing plastic overalls or layers of clothing. They roam the garden and friends' houses as soon as they are able to make friends. Nordic children are independent and trusted, since everyone looks out for your kids in the Nordics. Kids are allowed to be curious and get to know the world around them independently. And outdoor living in childhood does not stop there.

Kids as young as seven will cycle, walk or take public transport to school. This is nothing new. I used to take the bus on my own to school from day one. Kids are still allowed to play at school and there is a compulsory 15-minute break for every 45-minute learning period. Kids go outside for their break even if it is raining. Only when temperatures drop below -20°C are they allowed to stay inside.

Talk about using sisu! Being outdoors in the colder weather gives our children some resilience, but it is still nothing compared to kids in olden days skiing to school. Stories from grandparents about how they had to fight wolves on their way home stick in my memory. I'm not sure if it was true but it made me appreciate the fact that I was taking the bus not the skis!

 # Relationship with alcohol

You need a good constitution if you ever plan to visit the Nordics! Here, I will explore our relationship with alcohol. Do the Nordics have more alcohol problems than other countries?

Do we drink more than our neighbours? These are just a few of the many questions foreigners ask me when they hear where I am from.

There certainly is alcoholism in the Nordics. And like everywhere, we have our share of those who do not know when to stop. On average, though, this is no more than what you find in other European countries.

Alcohol in the Nordics

Alcohol use differs between the Nordic countries. We Finns are known to like beer and vodka, Swedes like lager and wine, and Norwegians love pilsner. Iceland's most famous drink has been a schnapps called brennivín also called 'black death' or 'burning wine' due to the high alcohol content.

The legal age to drink and buy alcohol is 18 in all the Nordic countries except Iceland where it is 20. In Norway, you need to be 20 to be able to buy spirits, but in the rest of the Nordics the age for purchasing most alcohol is 18. Interestingly, Denmark does not have a legal age for drinking, hence having the highest number of teenage drinkers in Europe. If you are 16, you can buy beer from a shop but no stronger than that. As you can see, the exact rules about alcohol sales are different from country to country.

Where you get alcohol

In Finland, you cannot buy hardcore vodka from supermarkets, only beer. Anything more, you need to go to Alko, the government off-licence chain that is permitted to sell stronger alcohol than average beer. Government control is tight, although you find Alko outlets in every small place.

In Iceland, the government regulated shop is called Vínbúðin, in Sweden, Systembolaget, and in Norway, Vinmonopolet. Denmark has no government-run off licences except in the Faroe Islands.

Home brew is another option as the cost of a pint of beer is expensive in the Nordics so many students go to the effort of brewing their own. In recent years, there has been growing momentum for gin distilleries, wineries or indie beer breweries in the Nordic countries. The climate change has been credited for the movement towards setting up smaller local gin distilleries and they have become popular.

Stories with alcohol

I recall underage drinking. When I was 16, I drank some wine with friends and had a huge headache the next day. On the day of my 18th birthday, I got to go to the local night club and of course I wanted to try all the drink I could. In the end, I got so drunk that I missed school the next day and my mum had to call in sick for me. I had alcohol poisoning, for sure. I did not touch alcohol for the next two years.

After that, I was put off by the smell of alcohol for a long time. Even today, I cannot have tequila as a result. The smell makes me want to puke. It was a good lesson about spirits, something that I have not forgotten.

Is my story unique? I do not think so. Many young Nordic people go through the baptism of drinking alcohol for the first time. They boast about the amount and age when they had their first drink to their friends.

Would the Nordics be better for having a more French-style alcohol culture where we introduce kids to alcohol earlier? You might think that the principle of alcohol being something you only drink with a meal is a good one, but alcohol consumption is actually higher in France than in Finland, partly due to more relaxed attitudes around drinking.

What could be done differently?

The preventative healthcare system in the Nordics supports education about the dangers of alcohol from school-age kids onwards. Are we missing something that would make more sense in the long term?

I am not sure that the answer to the alcohol question is easy, but I wonder if regulations truly work. Should there be a more co-operative version of control within families, youth workers and school to tackle the issues? If I look at myself and my friends from school, we did not end up having alcohol issues even if we did do it a lot in our youth, so perhaps tackling it socially is one way forward.

However, statistics show that young people today are increasingly turning to drugs and alcohol consumption is going down. For this generation, drugs are seen as the forbidden fruit and easily accessible. The numbers on drug abuse in all Nordic countries are high. Norway, Denmark and Sweden have high heroin overdose statistics. In Iceland, opioids are a problem, and buprenorphine and amphetamine are causing concern in Finland.

The bottom line is that we like to party in the Nordics. We drink more than our fair share of alcohol and there is no silver bullet for correcting the behaviour and trends associated with alcohol use. Be warned...if you visit the Nordics, you'll be expected to have the constitution for alcohol. As well as trying the variety of cuisines that you are offered, which is coming up next.

Nordic Cuisine

The cuisine in the Nordics is diverse. There is game from elk, hare and wild goose, as well as fish, prawns and everything in between. And yes, all the Nordic countries have their own version of the cinnamon bun or meatball recipe. I have included a few of my favourite recipes here for you to try out.

This was not supposed to be a cookbook, but good food is an integral part of who we are as Nordics. You can get a taste of the culture by having a cinnamon bun with your coffee or attempting more complex cooking like a sandwich cake or making meatballs from the scratch.

Lots of the food in the Nordics is based on what we have available around us. Yes, we have sushi bars but we love to make jams from different berries that are available in nature. Pickles and bread are usually part of every meal. You find these in most kitchens and there is variety of a pickled herring and many kinds of gherkins. Fish is the basis of many national dishes in the Nordic countries. From fermented shark or *hákarl* in Iceland, to salmon soup that is traditional in the Wild Taiga region in Finland, where I am from.

MEATBALLS

Party food the Nordic way or just a weekday dinner, this is the dish that Swedes have claimed as their national cuisine. Making the meatballs yourself is a skill and we tend to add some other spices like onion powder or paprika just to change the flavour a little bit, but it's your choice.

500g minced beef
1/4 cup breadcrumbs
2 tablespoons freshly chopped flat leaf parsley
1 tablespoon allspice
1 finely chopped white onion
2 tablespoon finely chopped garlic
Salt and pepper to taste
1 egg
1/4 cup parmesan cheese
Butter to brown the meatballs

Preparations

- In a medium-sized bowl, combine the ground beef, breadcrumbs, parsley, allspice, onion, garlic, salt and pepper, and egg. Mix well.

- Roll into 12 large meatballs or 20 small meatballs.

- Heat one tablespoon of butter.

- Add the meatballs and cook, turning continuously until brown on each side and cooked through. Transfer to a plate and cover with foil.

You can cook meatballs in the oven at 200°C for 15-20 minutes until no longer pink in the middle. Turn halfway through so the bottoms do not dry out.

THE BEST CINNAMON BUNS

Every Nordic country has their own name for cinnamon buns and every family has their own version of the recipe. This is how we make it at my house. It's a kids' favourite and most of them are gone before we get the last batch out of the oven.

6 cups white flour
2 eggs
200g melted butter
500 ml full fat milk or water
170g caster sugar
2.5 tablespoons dry yeast
3 tablespoon cardamom powder
Cinnamon
Room temperate soft butter
Sugar (white or brown)

Preparations

- Melt the yeast into the warm water or milk.
- Add the eggs, sugar, cardamom, and part of the flour.
- Knead dough until you can remove it from the bowl.
- Add the rest of the flour while kneading on a hard surface and then add the melted butter.
- Let the dough rise in a warm place until it is two times its size.
- Roll the dough into a square 60cm x 40cm and 1cm thick.
- Spread soft butter on top of the dough, dust with cinnamon covering the dough from edge to edge. Top it with sugar all over.
- Roll from the long edge until you form a roll and put the edge on the bottom.
- Cut the roll with a sharp knife on a triangular angle to make 30 equal slices.
- Lift the thinnest part of the slice up and press gently down with the blunt end of the knife.
- Let the buns rise under a towel for 20 minutes.
- Bake at 225°C for 5-10 minutes until golden brown.

LOHI VOILEIPÄKAKKU OR SMÖRGÅSTÅRTOR (SALMON SANDWICH CAKE)

Sandwich cakes are savoury cakes made using sliced bread as the cake base. Layers of fillings like mayonnaise, fish or meat, covered with vegetables like cucumber, carrot, dill and mayonnaise-based topping. Always a favourite for birthday parties and festive gatherings.

    1 cut loaf of white sandwich bread
    250 ml milk
    250 g hot smoked salmon
    2 large salted gherkins
    180 g cream cheese
    1 tablespoon lemon juice
    1 cup of fresh dill
    1/2 teaspoon fine black pepper
    180 g cream cheese
    150 g cold smoked salmon
    1 lemon
    Dill

Preparations

- Remove the crusts of the bread. Chop the warm smoked salmon in a bowl, dice the pickles and chop the dill. Mix the smoked salmon, salted gherkins, lemon juice, black pepper and dill together in a bowl with cream cheese.

- Line the bread pan (31cm x 9cm) with plastic wrap so that there is plenty left to fall over the sides.

- Press four slices of bread into the bottom of the pan. Moisten the loaves with milk and spread 1/3 of the smoked salmon filling on top. Repeat until all the filling is used.

- Place a layer of bread on top.

- Lift the edges of the plastic wrap over the cake and wrap the pan tightly. Put a cutting board or similar on top of the pan as a weight and let the sandwich cake firm up overnight in the fridge.

- Next day, spread the remaining cream cheese on the surface and sides of the sandwich cake.

- Cut the cold smoked salmon slices in half and slice the washed lemon.

- Garnish the cake with cold smoked salmon, lemon slices and dill.

Salmiakki aka salted liquorice

We cannot talk about Nordic cuisine without mentioning salmiakki or salmiak. The salted liquorice called salmiakki is only produced and eaten in the Netherlands, northern Germany and the Nordics.

The salty taste of this confectionery comes from ammonium chloride. The liquorice is usually black or a shade of grey or brown. Yes, we call it candy even if the taste is not for everyone.

The effects of salmiakki candy

Once you pop one in your mouth, your tongue starts to tingle. You get the salty sour taste followed by a sweeter afterburn. Your mouth starts to water, while feeling dry and thirsty. You spit the candy out! That is usually how foreigners experience salmiakki.

We love to give this delicacy to our foreign friends when they visit. My husband has been surprised by it many times on his trips to Finland. He cannot understand how we can create so many things containing *salmiakki*. There's *salmiakki* ice cream, chocolate, bread, biscuits, meat, donuts, vodka, soap and even *salmiakki* marinated chicken wings. You name it, we have produced it with this delicious salty-tasting sweet. You either love it or hate it. Mainly you are confused by how this stuff can be called candy when it is so foul!

My podcast guests have commented on the gross-tasting black liquorice and I recall Japanese expatriate Daiki Yoshikawa's reaction to tasting the sweet for the first time in Finland saying, "I could not finish it."

History of salmiakki

The fascination and love of the salmiakki started in the 1930s when it was first available in the shops. Before this, you could get it from the pharmacy only. Pharmacies produced their own cough medicine at the time. They added ammonium chloride to the mix to break down mucus. The cough medicine tasted like salted liquorice.

Perhaps this explains the creation of the famous *apteekin salmiakki* (pharmacy salmiakki*)* that you can still buy in Finland. I recall from my childhood that you could only get this stuff from the pharmacy. It was measured on a little white paper cup and sold by weight. These little black diamond shape *salmiakki* were delicious and are still available from candy stores today.

Why do Nordics love this candy? Well, it is something different and we all learn to eat it in childhood. This might be something to do with Viking heritage too, as they used to use salt to preserve fish, meat and much more. However, I am told that people in Iceland are not that keen on *salmiakki*. When in Finland, though, you can find the shelves full of different kinds of salty liquorice from sweet to sour to spicy. Heaven for me!

What salmiakki should you try?

No wonder Finns are said to be the heaviest consumers of candies with 14kg per year per person. And men consume salmiakki more than women.

The most popular ones are the Turkish Peber by Fazer, but you can find candy shops with a huge selection of *salmiakki* and other candies in every little town. You can buy these by weight just shovelling the candies into your paper bag and making your own mixture.

There is a risk of high blood pressure if you eat too much. Although liquorice does not come with a health warning, pregnant women are recommended to avoid them in Finland.

The fact is *salmiakki* tells us something about the Nordic psyche. You need to be a tough Viking to survive the weather... and to eat some *salmiakki*, you need to be even tougher!

 # Final Thoughts

When I started writing this book, I wanted to take you on a journey of what it is to come from the Nordics. I wanted to show you what you can learn from the Nordic countries and cultures, as well as how to implement that in your own life.

I hope this little book has answered your questions about Nordic lifestyle and made you even more curious about what the Nordics have to offer. Perhaps your next trip will be to the Nordics? As I am writing this, I am long overdue a trip to Finland, as it has been two years since the start of the pandemic and four years since I went back to the Nordics.

If I were to summarise the best way to have a little bit of slow Nordicness in your life, I would say:

- Have a fika, a cup of coffee and bun with a friend.
- Get cosy and have a hygge moment listening to music and reading this book.
- When life gets hard, pull out your sisu inner strength to get through.
- Sprinkle happiness around you, show gratitude towards people and help someone out.
- Take a walk in nature to feel refreshed and rejuvenated.
- Put some plastic in the recycling and make sustainable living part of your life.

Part of Nordic happiness is about these little things, but mostly we Nordics feel *togetherness* with each other. Being similar due to language, culture and sharing borders makes us more appreciative of the people we know we can rely on. Perhaps this is what we Nordic people do best: get to know our neighbours.

I would never have learned to appreciate my culture, background and heritage if I had not moved overseas. For me, living in Australia has crystallised the common factors I can see between Nordic people and the way we look out for each other.

We could all use a little of the Nordic togetherness to help us tackle the challenges life throws at us. We can all be kinder and do better by having more understanding of our neighbours and perhaps adopting some of their habits. Understanding creates harmony and that leads to happiness.

Nordic facts and figures

COFFEE Finns consume 12 kg per person of coffee annually. That is 1,100 cups of coffee each every year! The rest of the Nordics are not far behind this either. Norwegians consume 9.9 kg per person per year; Sweden 7.8 kg; Denmark 8.7 kg and Iceland 8.9 kg. We love to have hot drinks. Mainly coffee. With milk.

MILK Finland has the highest per capita milk consumption in the world. It goes well with the coffee so... no espresso in Finland!

ARE THERE MORE LAKES THAN PEOPLE IN FINLAND? Although there are millions of lakes in Finland and the other Nordic countries, people are not outnumbered. There are over 1 million lakes against 5.5 million people.

ICE CREAM Finland consumes ice cream more than any other Nordic country. There is no difference in ice cream consumption in summer or winter. My hubby laughed about this on his first Finnish visit when he was given ice cream after breakfast.

Juhannus / *Midsommar* / Sankthansaften (Midsummer)
Summer Solstice celebrations around 24 June in the Nordics.

Kantele
Finnish plucking folk instrument.

Koselig (*koosh-lee*)
Norwegian word for being cosy, rather together as a group of friends than alone. In other words, the Norwegian word for hygge.

Lagom (*laa-gum*)
Having just enough, not too little, not too much. This Swedish concept sums up how the Nordics are happy just as they are.

Lykke (*loo-kah*)
Danish word for happiness and joy.

Midsommarstång (Midsummer pole)
A Swedish maypole about 6m (20 feet) tall with two large hoops at the top. Many say it originated as a symbol of fertility but the actual origins are unknown.

Mifu
Meat alternative made of milk protein.

Mysig (*muu-sik*)
Swedish word for being cosy, comfortable and agreeable. Giving someone a mysig smile is the Swedes' version of describing a lovely moment.

Nisse / Tompte / Tonttu
Small garden gnome type creature.

Nyckelharpa
Swedish traditional violin-like instrumeent.

Pantsdrunk / Kalsarikännit (*kalsari-kaen-it*)
Being a homebody, drinking alone until you pass out on your sofa after spending the evening bitching about your work.

Pesäpallo
Finnish game equivalent to baseball.

Polser
Danish for the hotdog eaten on constitution day.

Salmiakki / Salmiak (*salmi ak:i*)
Salted liquorice that we call candy, but you might call weird.

Sauna / Bastu (*sau-na*)
Describes a room with a heating element and rocks. Water is poured on these rocks to create a high temperature and steam. You find different saunas throughout the Nordic countries. The word sauna is from Finnish, but bastu is used in other Nordic countries as well.

Savu (*sa-vu*)
Smoke used to cure meats and fish in the Nordics. There is also savu sauna that has no chimney. The wood is burned in a large stove and smoke is

allowed to fill the entire sauna room. Once the fire is put out or allowed to die, the smoke is ventilated out and the heat left keeps the sauna warm.

Sisu (*si-su*)
Finnish word for grit, courage or inner strength.

Syttende Mai
Norwegian national day on 17 May every year.

Utepils (*Ooh-ta-pilz*)
The Norwegians have a great word for having a beer outdoors. Ute means outside and pils means pilsner or lager.

Yoik/Joik
Yoiks are song-chants and are traditionally sung a cappella, usually slowly and deep in the throat.

Image credits

CHAPTER 1
4 Sixteen Miles Out, **6** Maria Vojtovicova, **8** Designed by pch.vector/Freepik, **10-11** Mika, **12** Tobias Tullius, **14-15** Designed by Freepik, **17** Mika Luoma, **18** Christer Gundersen, **20** Designed by pch.vector/Freepik, **21** Priscilla du Preez, **22-23** Tapio Haaja, **26-27** Valdemaras, **28** Amy Asher

CHAPTER 2
32-33 Febiyan, **35** Mark Konig, **36, 38,39** Shutterstock, **40** Beatriz Miller **43-44** Philip Myrtorp, **46, 47, 49** Wikipedia, **50** Nikola Johnny Mirkovic, **52-53** Gregorio Nuti, **54-55** Designed by Olga_spb/Freepik, **61** Designed by pch.vector/Freepik

CHAPTER 3
62-63 Maria, **65** Elena Kloppenburg, **68-69** Karoline Vargdal, **71, 75** Shutterstock, **78** Freepik, **79** Kylie Cheung, **81** M Wrona, **85** Thomas Tucker, **88** Nick Kane, **94** Jisca Lucia, **97** Jeff Finley, **99** Radek Jedynak

CHAPTER 4
100-101 Saikrishna Saketh Yellapragada, **104-105** iStock, **108** Pikisuperstar/Freepik, **111** Maria Ilves, **115** @macrovector/Freepik, **118** Kelly Sikkema, **120** Designed by Freepik, **123** Sixteen Miles Out, **127** Vecteezy, **129** Jason Leung, **130** Helena Lopes, **131** Rina Kustova

CHAPTER 5
136-137 Giu Vicente, **138** Priscilla du Preez, **140** Daphne Richard, **143** Josue Michel, **145** Designed by pch.vector/Freepik, **146** Lindsay Cotter, **149** Mark Stosberg, **150** Annie Spratt, **156** Designed by pikisuperstar/Freepik, **158** Shutterstock, **160** Stockbroker, 123rf

CHAPTER 6
164 Ethan Hoover, **168-169** Janko Ferlic, **173** Nordic Mum, **178** Vecteezy

Thank you for reading

Thanks for reading! If you loved the book and have a moment to spare, I would really appreciate a short **review** as this helps new readers find my books. Just jump to the platform that you purchased this book from.

I love hearing from my readers, and I love having conversation about all things Nordic. Join my email list **https://www. subscribepage.com/b6v5z1**. I will give a **FREE audio** about how the *Nordic Lifestyle* book came about and more background about myself so you can get to you know me better.

I promise not to spam you but keep you updated on what is happening in my world and what I am writing next.

Thank you,
Susanna H

To my sons Luke and Leo who inspire everything that I do. And to my husband Mike who never says no to my even sometimes bad ideas. Thank you for saying yes to this book.

Acknowledgements

Kris Emery Editorial My editor who landed on this journey for a purpose to get the information about Nordics before her trip to Norway. She really was in the right place at the right time. Cannot say how much this book improved because of her editing and feedback. Thank you Kris!

Bea Reis Custodio My designer who really got what I meant from the get go. The cover is a real reflection of what I was trying to achieve and all that Nordic represent to me. Loved working with you Bea!

My Beta Readers Yes you, who read my book and gave me feedback before I hit publish. It was all much appreciated and I loved the feedback and corrections that made this book better because of it.

Thank you to my family and friends, who had been hearing about this book for ages... I promise the next one will be faster. But just giving feedback, pointers and just listening to my ramblings at times was all so much appreciated.

To all my readers, listeners of my podcast *The Nordic Mum*, and people on my email list who have sent me line or two as encouragement over the past year THANK YOU!

Yes there will be another one so watch this space...

References

The Nordic Mum Blog and Podcast Episodes

Daiki Yoshikawa podcast episode: How to Find Happy Scandinavian Life *https://www.thenordicmum. com/how-to-find-happy-scandinavian-life/*

Nicola Capper podcast episode: When Unexpectant Gift Leads You To Nordic Design *https://www.thenordicmum. com/loving-the-nordic-design/*

Ingrid Opstad podcast episode: How to Find Happy Scandinavian Life *https://www.thenordicmum. com/how-to-find-happy-scandinavian-life/*

Sisu the Finnish Art of Courage podcast episode *https://www.thenordicmum. com/sisu-the-finnish-art-of-courage/*

Why Finnish Schools are Different podcast episode *https://www.thenordicmum. com/episode-48-why-finnish-schools-are-different/*

7 Surprising Facts About Sweden podcast episode *https://www.thenordicmum. com/surprising-facts-about-sweden/*

All About Scandinavian Design.

How to Have Hygge Lifestyle with a Budget

How to Hygge and Decluttering Your Life

How to Have Hyggelig Time with Your Kids

What is the Meaning of These Nordic Words

How to Have Sisu in Your Life

Friluftsliv: Is this the Answer to Enjoying Winter More?

Further reading about the Nordics

Little Book of Hygge by Meik Weiking

Lagom The Swedish Art of Balancing Life by Linnea Dunne

Little Book of Lykke by Meik Weiking

Sisu The Finnish Art of Courage by Joanne Nylund

The Little Book of Fika by Lynda Balsev

The Year of Living Danishly by Helen Russell

Koselig- The Norwegian Concept that Will Help You Though Winter

Polarpedia

Spinnova

Nordic Council

Artek

Nordic fiction authors

Laura Linstedt

Jo Nesbo

Max Seeck

Sofi Oksanen

Leena Krohn

Helena Halme

Antti Tuomainen

Margit Abenius

Wilhelm Agrell

Annie Åkerhielm

Martin Allwood

Satu Rämö

Hjördis Piuva Andersson

Sauna

https://en.wikipedia.org/wiki/Giuseppe_Acerbi

https://www.nature.com/articles/s41371-017-0008-z

Nordic noir in television

The Killing (Danish)

The Bridge (Sweden)

Stieg Larsson's Millennium series (Sweden)

Acquitted (Norway)

Department Q (Denmark)

Case (Iceland)

Bordertown (Finland)

Trapped (Iceland)

Nordic real crime podcasts

True Crime Sweden

Evidence Locker True Crime

True Crime Finland

Nordic True Crime

Research about happiness and gender

https://www.weforum.org/reports/global-gender-gap-report-2021

https://worldhappiness.report/

https://www.europeansocialsurvey.org/

About the Author

Susanna Heiskanen is a Finnish mother of two who lives in Australia with her husband and sons. Susanna is an experienced podcaster and blogger. Nordic Lifestyle: Embrace Slow Living, Cultivate Happiness and Know When to Take Off Your Shoes is her debut book about her experiences and life in the Nordics. Susanna shows you how to live the simple Nordic lifestyle wherever you are. Her anecdotes about her life and experiences as a mother and a Finn are funny and poignant. She details how life is different in the Nordics... in a good way. So, take off your shoes, have a cup of coffee and a bun, and let Susanna show you how to add a little Nordicness to your life.

.

Made in the USA
Coppell, TX
26 May 2023